Building and Surveying Series

Accounting and Finance for Building and Surveying A. R. Jennings
Advanced Valuation Diane Butler and David Richmond
Applied Valuation, second edition Diane Butler
Asset Valuation Michael Rayner
Auctioning Real Property R. M. Courtenay Lord
Building Economics, fourth edition Ivor H. Seeley
Building Maintenance, second edition Ivor H. Seeley
Building Procurement, second edition Alan E. Turner
Building Quantities Explained, fifth edition Ivor H. Seeley
Building Services George Hassan
Building Surveys, Reports and Dilapidations Ivor H. Seeley
Building Technology, fifth edition Ivor H. Seeley
Civil Engineering Quantities, sixth edition Ivor H. Seeley and George P. Murray
Commercial Lease Renewals – A Practical Guide Philip Freedman and Eric F. Shapiro
Construction Contract Claims Reg Thomas
Construction Economics: An Introduction Stephen L. Gruneberg
Construction Marketing – Strategies for Success Richard Pettinger
Construction Planning, Programming and Control Brian Cooke and Peter Williams
Economics and Construction Andrew J. Cooke
Environmental Science in Building, fourth edition R. McMullan
Facilities Management, second edition Alan Park
Greener Buildings: Environmental Impact of Property Stuart Johnson
Introduction to Building Services, second edition E. F. Curd and C. A. Howard
Introduction to Valuation, third edition David Richmond
JCT Standard Form of Building Contract, 1998 edition Richard Fellows and Peter Fenn
Measurement of Building Services George P. Murray
Principles of Property Investment and Pricing, second edition W. D. Fraser
Property Development: Appraisal and Finance David Isaac
Property Finance David Isaac
Property Investment David Isaac
Property Management: a Customer-Focused Approach Gordon Edington
Property Valuation Techniques David Isaac and Terry Steley
Public Works Engineering Ivor H. Seeley
Quantity Surveying Practice, second edition Ivor H. Seeley
Real Estate in Corporate Strategy Marion Weatherhead
Recreation Planning and Development Neil Ravenscroft
Small Building Works Management Alan Griffith
Sub-Contracting under the JCT Standard Forms of Building Contract Jennie Price
Urban Land Economics and Public Policy, fifth edition P. N. Balchin, G. H. Bull
  and J. L. Kieve

By the same author

The Valuation of Property Investments (with N. Enever) [Estates Gazette]
Property Companies: Share Price and Net Asset Value (with N. Woodroffe)
    [Greenwich University Press]
Urban Economics: A Global Perspective (with P. N. Balchin and J. Chen) [Palgrave]

Building and Surveying Series
Series Standing Order
ISBN 0–333–71692–2 hardcover
ISBN 0–333–69333–7 paperback
(outside North America only)

You can receive future titles in this series as they are published by placing a standing order. Please contact your bookseller or, in the case of difficulty, write to us at the address below with your name and address, the title of the series and the ISBN quoted above.

Customer Services Department, Macmillan Distribution Ltd
Houndmills, Basingstoke, Hampshire RG21 6XS, England

Property Valuation Principles

David Isaac
Professor of Real Estate Management
Head of Property and Land Management
University of Greenwich

palgrave

First published 2002 by
PALGRAVE
Houndmills, Basingstoke, Hampshire RG21 6XS and
175 Fifth Avenue, New York, N.Y. 10010
Companies and representatives throughout the world

PALGRAVE is the new global academic imprint of
St. Martin's Press LLC Scholarly and Reference Division and
Palgrave Publishers Ltd (formerly Macmillan Press Ltd).

ISBN 0–333–92114–3

This book is printed on paper suitable for recycling and made from fully managed and sustained forest sources.

A catalogue record for this book is available from the British Library.

10   9   8   7   6   5   4   3   2   1
11   10   09   08   07   06   05   04   03   02

Printed and bound in Great Britain by
Creative Print & Design (Wales), Ebbw Vale

Contents

Preface

This book is intended to provide an introduction to property valuation. The general approach is that property appraisal is the overall aim, and that this is divided into market valuation and investment analysis. It is in the area of market valuation that this text concentrates. The book covers five areas of study:

- valuation and markets;
- methods of valuation;
- the investment method in detail;
- taxation and statutory valuations;
- the development appraisal and finance.

The intention is to discuss the context of the market, show how valuation practice has developed within this context and explain the application of valuation methods in practice.

The book will be useful for both students and practitioners. For students it will provide a text at initial level (first/second year undergraduates) in estate management, property, surveying, planning, design and construction disciplines. Those in adjacent areas of study, such as housing and economics, will find it a useful introduction to the area of property valuation. Practitioners involved with property and real estate, and this includes a wide area of professionals, including surveyors, builders, construction managers, architects, engineers, estate managers and agents, will also find it a useful overview. Professional advisers, such as bankers, financial advisers, accountants, investors, analysts and lawyers, should also find this text useful as an aid to their dealings in the property sector.

I have aimed to reference the material as fully as possible but apologise for any omissions. There are relatively few texts in the area of property compared to most other investment sectors, and I have tried to reference existing ones as completely as possible in order to provide additional views and perspectives for the reader. Where possible, spreadsheet analysis has been used to explain and assist in the calculations. Each chapter has the overall aims set out at the beginning and also includes a summary at the end. Key terms are explained and exercise questions are included in relevant sections.

Finally, I would like to thank those who have assisted me in writing this book, especially Christopher Glennie, my publisher, who has been patient with my progress and supportive in the book's development. I would also like to thank Terry Steley and Mark Daley of the University of Greenwich for their help and observations on the book. Finally, as ever, I am reliant on the continued support of the management and staff of the School of Land and Construction Management at the University of Greenwich in developing my studies and research, and I am grateful for their help.

As a result of studying this book, students should attain the following objectives:

- an understanding of property appraisal (valuation and analysis) in the context of property markets;
- an understanding and ability to use the principal methods of valuation;
- an understanding of the application of valuations in a variety of investment and development contexts;
- an ability to relate techniques of appraisal to a wider economic context based on property development, finance and the financial management of property projects.

David Isaac

University of Greenwich
School of Land and Construction Management
April 2001

Acknowledgements

The author and publisher wish to thank those who have assisted in providing data and published sources. Every effort has been made to trace all the copyright holders, but if any have been inadvertently overlooked, the publishers will be pleased to make the necessary arrangements at the first opportunity.

Part 1:
Valuation and Markets

1 The Concept of Property Valuation

1.1 **Principles of property investment**
1.2 **Property appraisal: market valuation and investment analysis**
1.3 **Prices and values**
1.4 **Traditional property valuation**

AIMS AND OBJECTIVES

This chapter introduces the principles of property investment; the key aspects of investment and a summary of the property context in which the investment takes place. It then goes on to examine property markets and the distinction between the concept of price and value within those markets. It concludes by beginning to apply the concepts and principles to an investment valuation.

1.1 PRINCIPLES OF PROPERTY INVESTMENT

Introduction

A property or building can be owner-occupied or rented, the latter being an investment property. It may of course be vacant, resulting from being surplus to the owner's requirements or a poor investment! A large proportion of property is owner-occupied but most of the conventional texts and theories in property are applied to the investment market. The investment market for property cannot be seen in isolation from other investment markets. The application of funds to property has to reflect competition from other forms of investment. The decision to invest in a particular area will be a comparison of return and security, and thus knowledge of alternative investments and their analysis could be very important. The application of financial techniques to property investment can also be important and this can clearly be seen in the securitisation and unitisation of property, which is a key area of development in property investment. Another important point to be made concerns the nature of the lender and

3

the property to which finance is applied. At its simplest, the financial arrangement may deal with an individual purchasing a single property with a single loan, but it is usually more complex. Finance is generally raised by corporate entities, such as property companies, using existing property and other assets as collateral for the purchase of a portfolio of assets which may include property assets but not exclusively. Finally, it is important to realise the significance of property and property investment to the economy. This importance can be shown in three different ways: as a factor of production, as a corporate asset and as an investment medium. As a factor of production, property provides the space in which economic activity and production take place, and the efficiency and costs of such space will affect the cost of goods and services produced. As a corporate asset, property forms the major part of asset values in companies' balance sheets and the majority of corporate debt is secured against it. As an investment, it is one of the major types of investment held by individual investors and the financial institutions on which pensions and assurance benefits depend (Fraser, 1993).

Three particular aspects of this process need to be distinguished: valuation, ownership and value.

• *Property valuation*
Valuation is a means of providing an assessment of the capital value of, or the income arising from a property investment. There is a range of possible investment opportunities from works of art through oil futures and gold to shares, government stocks and property. The point of investment is that it provides the investor with an income, growth in capital value of the investment, or both. Thus investment involves an initial payment (a capital outlay) so that an income can be received in the future over a period of time.

• *Property ownership*
Property investment is different from other types of investment in that ownership of physical assets like land and buildings is far more complex than the ownership of a share certificate. It also involves the owner in more responsibility and obligations than other forms of investment.

• *Economic value*
Land is a scarce resource and its supply is limited. Land can change its use to increase supply in the short-term but in the long-term it is fixed. Expensive projects such as land reclamation or the possibilities of extra-terrestrial colonisation are feasible but the effect on the overall supply of land would be marginal. Value, as related to land, was of great interest to the classical economists who perceived that the supply of land was fixed. They therefore used the concept of economic rent to describe payments not only to

land but also to any factor involved in the production process which was unable to adjust to its supply and thus able to achieve a higher price because of its position of scarcity.

Property valuation

The concept of value is a difficult one to comprehend. Economists relate it to utility but this is not of any practical use when determining actual values in the market. A price may be determined on the market but this may not always equate with the valuation of the property in the market. Problems of the difference of price and valuation arise because the marketplace for property is decentralised and fragmented. For instance, you can ascertain the price of your shares from the morning papers but the price of an office building might be more difficult to determine. It may be that an identical office block has just been sold and this should tell you the price of the block you are looking at. It should do, but it often does not. The problem is one of imperfect markets in that the transaction may be difficult to reconstruct, and it could also be that the outside parties have limited knowledge of the deal that was actually struck. There is a wide range of reasons why premises are bought and sold, and the environment in which transactions are taking place is constantly changing.

Besides the problem of assessing a price of a property, there is also a problem of assessing value when a property is not being sold and a transaction does not actually take place. The property could be valued for a number of reasons that do not involve a purchase or sale; for mortgage, compulsory purchase or tax reasons, for instance. These valuations do not necessarily lead to a transaction that can support or contradict the valuation. Thus the value of the property is not exact and it is often adjusted according to the purpose for which it is used. The negotiated price is dependent on the particular circumstances of the transaction and certainly on whether you are buying or selling.

Property investment markets

The market for commercial property is an established investment market but because there is no central market place and because each property is unique, there is a difficulty in understanding how the market works. This is compounded by the fact that information on the products in the market and the nature of transactions is restricted; information is passed by word of mouth rather than being properly documented in the press or in published reports. The actual detail of the transaction in the market, the details of rents passing, the nature of the lease terms agreed and the yield used in any capital transaction may remain confidential. Thus the property market could be a dangerous place for the ordinary person to invest in because of lack of market information.

The characteristics of property markets have been summarised as shown in Box 1.1.

One of the most important points about property investment is the holding of property in a portfolio of investments with other major asset classes that are government securities (gilts or bonds), company shares (equities) and cash. Investors will not hold just one type of asset but will diversify so as 'not to have all their eggs in one basket'. This means that any investment analysis that concentrates on one investment or even one type of investment will be incorrect. It is the range of investments that needs to be considered and the effect that one investment has on another. If an investor has investments A and B in a portfolio and is then offered C, it is

---

BOX 1.1: THE CHARACTERISTICS OF PROPERTY MARKETS (adapted from Darlow, 1983)

- The market is fragmented, poorly recorded, secretive and generally unregulated.
- There is no central agency or institution (such as Lloyds insurance for the insurance industry).
- There is no physical focal point.
- It is difficult to find average figures for property transactions or provide an appropriate sample in order to provide some statistical analysis that would help in understanding property.
- The market is diverse and complex in nature.
- There are national, regional and local variations to the market. Property markets tend to be localised, disorganised and vary in classification (such as geographical location, type of property, quality of property, value and size of investment).
- There is an imperfect knowledge of the market and within the market there is no central price or listing (such as on-line prices, as there are for the transaction of stocks and shares).
- There is no central registry of transactions which is complete.
- The market tends to favour monopoly, because the supply of land does not respond easily to changes in demand.
- There is no freedom of entry and exit from the market because of locational, legal, financial, taxation and other constraints.

the effect on the overall portfolio by adding *C* that is critical, rather than its own characteristics. *C* could be a very risky property but experience tells us that if its changes in value are different from those of assets *A* and *B*, then its inclusion in the portfolio might make the portfolio less risky. In considering the structure of the portfolio, one should also consider the correlation of returns in property with other asset classes. Brown (1991) carried out research into the relationship of property returns to other asset classes. In the period January 1979–December 1982, he found that property portfolios exhibited a low and negative correlation with gilts. As the holding period of investments increases so does the correlation coefficient, suggesting greater relationship. There is a negative relationship between properties and the FT All Share Index; the relationship with the property share index is much higher and increases with the holding period. A high correlation between property and the Retail Price Index (RPI) indicates the ability of property to act as a hedge (an insurance) against inflation.

In 1988 Richard Ellis also carried out research to show that the property market moves in an opposite manner to equities and gilts, and is thus a good prospect for the diversification of a portfolio. This study found:

(i) **very limited similarity** between property returns and equities (shares);
(ii) **no similarity** between property returns and gilts (government stocks);
(iii) gilts and equity returns were **more in line** (Barter, 1988).

The comparative performance of property against other assets over the period 1980–96 and forecast for the period 1996–2000 is shown in Figure 1.1 (Lennox, 1996). In the period 1980–95 it can be seen that property performed badly against equities and bonds (gilts). This performance should reflect the relationship between risk and return. Investments that have a greater risk should offer a higher return. Bonds are low in risk and we would expect low returns. Equities are considered more risky than property. Here you can see that property has not performed very well in the period 1980–95, as we would expect the property return to reflect the risk and therefore be between equities and bonds. In fact it performed worse. Although this analysis was carried out in 1996 and is now dated, the argument was that, in 1996, property would outperform the other asset classes and in 1996–2000 the anticipation was that the return would be more in line with the risk profiles of the asset classes.

If one takes away the sentiment of owning land and buildings, and this is a strong one, then a property investment is basically a flow of income arising from a property asset. This income may be distributed in many different ways to offer investors differing degrees of risk and differing returns. This is the basis of property securitisation and the innovative forms of property finance which have been developed. These new financial techniques

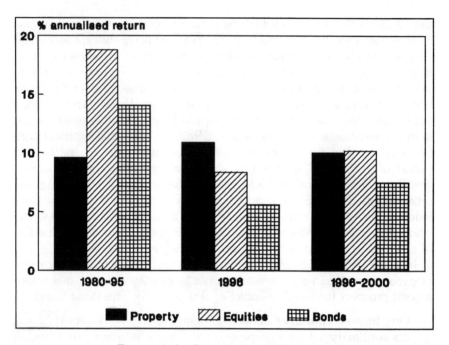

Figure 1.1 *Comparative performance*

attempt to overcome property's inherent illiquidity and inflexibility. But according to Barter (1988), the key concerns about property as an investment medium remain.

Illiquidity

Properties take 3 months to buy and sell. There is no certainty of price and terms until contracts are exchanged. This problem is acute for properties with capital values above £20 million because of the relatively small supply of potential single purchasers in the market, especially when there are no international purchasers. There are problems in appraising and financing the more substantial developments.

Inflexibility

There is a high unit cost with property purchases and little flexibility in the purchase; one needs to buy the whole. There are problems in portfolio diversification and management here. Property shares and property units offer some opportunity to diversify but property companies are taxed in the same way as other companies, and unauthorised property unit trusts are only available to pension funds and certain types of charities and cannot be listed. Now there are authorised trusts for the general public but these may remain unlisted and have a corporation tax liability on the income. Some of the problems of illiquidity and inflexibility have been addressed by 'swapping' properties in matched deals. This avoids the exposure and bad publicity of putting properties up for sale in a poor market. An example in 1996, for instance, was a swap valued at £34.35 million in which the Provident Mutual sold a mixed portfolio of six office, retail and industrial property to Allied London in exchange for eight retail warehouses, valued at £21.6 million, together with £12.75 million in cash.

Growth of debt finance

There has been a substantial increase in bank lending to the property sector in recent years. This has replaced new equity investment by institutions, especially in the 1980s, and the banks' over-lending encouraged the boom and subsequent slump at the beginning of the 1990s in the UK. Banks were also evident in the Japanese economic 'bubble' largely based on property and bank lending on property; this bubble burst at the time the property market collapsed in the UK in the early 1990s. Debt finance, used in an appropriate structure, can affect the return on equity owned, and the use of financial gearing to achieve this is described in a later chapter on finance.

Valuation methodology and precision

Conventional valuation methods are inflexible. The all-risk approach of traditional valuation methods is difficult to apply to more illiquid properties such as major shopping centres and substantial office buildings. A number of cases reflecting errors in the valuation of hotels and restaurants also confirm this. Conventional valuations also have difficulty in the valuation of over-rented property where rents are expected to fall on review.

The future role of the property profession

The liberalisation of the financial markets and the increased importance of debt in property funding require new competencies for chartered surveyors. The demands of the Financial Services Act for those providing information on finance and funding will require different and greater competence in the financial area. In this area and others, the professional institutions are reorienting themselves to the market. The RICS has adopted 'An Agenda for Change' and is determined to upgrade the status of property professionals in the UK.

Short-termism

Property is a long-term investment and cannot compete on similar terms with investments that pay off on a much shorter time horizon. Recent attitudes of funders and managers of companies in the UK indicate a short-term approach to investment and performance that is a reflection of the recent difficult economic times in which these companies have had to operate. Companies may in some cases have opted for very short-term investment appraisals and rapid payback. The pressure to perform well has not only led fund managers to increase their activity in managing funds but also led to a short-term perspective for investment. This strategy focuses on the short-term performance of companies in arriving at the valuation of a company's worth with emphasis on current profit performance and dividend payments. This perspective, suggested by Pike and Neale (1993), has many consequences across the spectrum of companies including:

(i) the neglect of the long-term by management, leading to a failure to undertake important long-term investments in resources and research and development;

(ii) the volatility of short-term corporate results becoming exaggerated in securities markets, producing unacceptable fluctuations in share prices.

Because of its long-term production cycle, these consequences are likely to be very damaging to property and construction. A survey carried out by the Department of Industry's Innovation Advisory Board in 1990 concluded that City influence on corporate activity led to companies prioritising short-term profits and dividends at the expense of research and development and other innovative investment. The survey also commented that the practices of the key financial institutions have sustained these priorities. Researchers in the USA have concluded that increasing shareholder power of institutional investors has had a damaging effect on research and development expenditure among US firms. The financiers of the City of London reject this criticism by saying that much of the responsibility for the lack of long-term innovation investment is attributable to company management. Specifically, they say it is managers' preference for growth by acquisition, their poor record of commercial development and their reward systems based on short-term targets (Pike and Neale, 1993). The implications for property in this respect are very clear, because property development and the development of its associated transport, social and services infrastructure are a long-term project. Development and refurbishment underpin the property investment market. Projects on difficult town centre sites or involving major infrastructure works encounter problems of risk and uncertainty as they extend into the future. Then there are the problems of high transfer cost and illiquidity in property; to force a sale of a development or investment property at an inappropriate time, for instance half way through a building contract, could cause a collapse in the price of the asset. This effect is accentuated because of the location attributes of property; markets are localised and imperfect.

The problem of short-termism is that such an attitude is inappropriate to property investment and finance where long-term strategies and returns are the key to successful projects.

1.2 PROPERTY APPRAISAL: MARKET VALUATION AND INVESTMENT ANALYSIS

Property appraisal (see Figure 1.2) consists of:

- *Market valuation;*
- *Investment analysis.*

Market valuation is the estimate of the possible exchange value in the market, the price at which the property will be sold.

- It is an estimate made before the transaction takes place.
- It is based on a valuer's knowledge of local market conditions and transactions.
- It requires:
  - knowledge of market data;
  - the context in which market transactions are being made;
  - the basis of the calculations used in the market to assess the market value.

The important element here is what the market judges to be the transaction price, not what a particular investor believes is a fair price or worth.

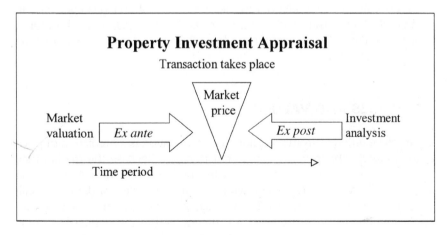

Figure 1.2 *Market valuation and investment analysis*

Prices in the market should be the product of supply and demand for a particular property. This is the same as other goods for which there are market transactions. There is a current debate as to whether the market is efficient or not, whether prices on the market actually reflect the knowledge in the market. There can be distortions or inefficiencies in the market at a particular time; an **arbitrageur** is a dealer in investments who will exploit these inefficiencies. The arbitrageur will buy low and resell having discovered that, in his view, a particular investment is being sold below its realistic price.

Investment analysis is the assessment of worth of an investment. The analysis takes place after the transaction has occurred. The returns arising on the investment can be assessed for a number of reasons:

• they can be compared with the price paid of the investment;
• a return can be assessed which can be net of tax;
• a return can be discounted using an appropriate rate for the investor – if a target rate is say 10 per cent then the return can be assessed as the element above the target rate;
• the comparison of the worth of the property with the price can be used to assess whether the investment was over-priced or under-priced on the market;
• the target rate could be considered a normal profit in economic terms – the additional return could be a supernormal profit;
• the assessment of worth can be calculated for an individual's requirements, which means that an individual's risk profile, tax position and target rate of return can be put into the calculation;
• the appraisal can be adjusted to take into account changes over time in the cash flows arising – discount rates can be changed, and risk profiles, growth rates and depreciation can be built in as well as breaks in income and rent reviews.

1.3   PRICES AND VALUES

Price will be different from valuation, as the valuation is a prediction of price in the market. This prediction may not transpire because the market may have inefficiencies or may change in the period when the value is being assessed. The value may also be wrong because insufficient data are available or because the data have been analysed incorrectly or an inappropriate technique has been used. Price is determined in the market by supply and demand. As in microeconomic theory, problems arise in the property market because the supply of land is essentially fixed and thus the supply is unable to adjust to changes in the demand. This lack of adjustment can lead to the price discrepancies described earlier.

Value to an individual investor may differ from the market view; the market view is an aggregation but an individual's view may be different. This could be for a number of different reasons; as we have seen, the tax difference could mean a different net-of-tax return or there could be non-economic considerations – fashion or personal taste or prejudice. Value is based on an economic concept of utility and this will differ from individual to individual. Alternative views of forecasts in the future will affect value; an investor concerned about future events will discount future income streams at a higher rate than will an investor with a more optimistic view. Value will also differ according to the investor's positioning in the market; for instance, the site being valued might be adjacent to an existing site already owned and therefore have an enhanced value; interests may be merged in a property to enhance value; properties can provide access or ransom strips for other development.

Economic concepts of value include suggestions of **exchange value** (price), **investment value** (worth) and **use value** (basically, use as existing, not redeveloped and not sold).

1.4 TRADITIONAL PROPERTY VALUATION

This chapter has examined some concepts related to value, and in this section applications of the terms used in traditional property valuations are introduced. This section deals with concepts of rates of interest and yields, and goes on to apply these in the basic methods of valuation

Rates of interest and yields

A yield is important to an investor; it indicates the level of earnings and it defines money earned over a time period. If 20 per cent is the yield of an investment, this means that £20 is earned for every £100 invested. If the yield is 5 per cent, then £5 is earned. Thus 20 per cent as a yield is obviously more attractive, but the concept is more complicated because the yield also indicates the risk of the investment. Risk is important; some investments involve greater risk than others do, so a higher return is offered on riskier investments to tempt investors away from safe investments. As an example, in drug smuggling, the risk is high and returns are very high. As an outsider in a horserace, the risk of not winning is high, say 100 to 1 odds. The payback period is a critical element in investment analysis. Yields can be compared simply using payback period analysis. A 20 per cent yield on £100 is £20 p.a.; the purchase cost of £100 is therefore paid back in 5 years (£100/£20 p.a. = 5 years) and this is the payback period. So at a 5 per cent yield, the payback period is 20 years. Risky investments tend to have an earlier payback period; there is an early recoupment of the original investment and the rest is profit. This approach ignores the time-preference value of money, that is £1 is worth more now than in 1 year's time. The yield that we expect from a property investment will be determined by a number of factors; a greater risk will mean a higher yield and vice versa. The investor will want the highest yield that can be obtained from any one investment, and there is therefore a need to look at and compare yields from different investments.

Rates of interest are considered in this section in the context of nominal rates of interest. So, if a company sells stock to investors, it needs to have an interest rate to tempt investors, say 10 per cent. The investor will receive £10 for every £100 of stock owned. See Example 1.1.

Example 1.1: Nominal interest and market interest rates

At time of stock issue:

nominal rate of interest	**10% p.a.**
nominal price of stock	£100
thus return is	£10 p.a.

The price of the stock may start at this level but the price will change over a period and if the £10 p.a. return is still offered on the original £100 nominal value of the stock, the rate of interest will change:

price falls to	£80
return still offered	£10
rate of interest (yield) is	£10/£80 = **12.5% p.a.**

In the example, a £10 p.a. return is still being offered because it is based on the *par value* of the stock, par value being the original offer price. So the only time when the nominal rate of interest equals yield is at the date of issue. The price of the stock issued will go up and down according to market fluctuations but the nominal rate at which the stock is issued will be based on the base rates in the financial markets. This analysis gives a clear relationship between income, yield and capital value. If the rate of interest or yield is 10 per cent and the capital value of the investment is £100, then the expected income is £10 p.a. By working back from this calculation, if an investment produces an income of £10 p.a. and the investor requires a yield of 10 per cent p.a., the price paid by the investor is £100 and this is the basis of the investment method of valuation.

The investment method of property valuation

Most investors seek to obtain a return on their invested money either as an annual income or a capital gain; the investment method of valuation is traditionally concerned with the former. Where the investor has a known sum of money to invest on which a particular return is required, the income can be readily calculated from:

$$\text{Income} = \text{Capital} \times \frac{i}{100} \quad \text{where} \quad i = \text{Rate of return required}$$

For example, if £1,000 is to be invested with a required rate of return of 8 per cent, the income will be:

$$\text{Income} = £1,000 \times \frac{8}{100} = £80\,\text{p.a.}$$

In this type of problem the capital is known and the income is to be calculated. In the case of real property the income (rent) is known, either from the actual rent passing under the lease or is estimated from the lettings of similar comparable properties and the capital value usually is calculated. The formula above has to be changed so that the capital becomes the subject:

$$\text{Capital} = \text{Income} \times \frac{100}{i}$$

What capital sum should be paid for an investment producing £8,000 per annum if a return of 8 per cent is required?

$$\text{Capital} = £800 \times \frac{100}{8} = £10,000$$

This process is known as 'capitalising' the income, in other words converting an annual income into a capital sum. It is essential that the income capitalised is 'net', that is clear of any expenses incurred by the investor under the lease. Therefore the formula can be modified to:

$$C = NI \times \frac{100}{i} \quad \text{where} \quad \begin{array}{l} C = \text{Capital} \\ NI = \text{Net income} \\ i = \text{Rate of return} \end{array}$$

For given rates of return, $100/i$ will be constant, for example:

Rate of return	100/*i*
10%	10
8%	12.5
12%	8.33

This constant is known as the Present Value of £1 per annum, or more commonly in real property valuation, Year's Purchase (abbreviated to YP). The formula can thus be finally modified to:

$$C = NI \times YP$$

where C is the Capital value, NI is the Net income and YP is the Year's Purchase. The YP calculated by using $100/i$ will only apply to incomes received in perpetuity, which are those received from freehold interests let at a full market rent or rack rent. Incomes to be received for shorter periods use a YP which must be calculated using a more complex formula (although tables of constants are available – *Parry's Valuation* and *Investment Tables* are most commonly used (Davidson, 1989). The traditional approach mirrored by *Parry's Tables* was to assume that the rental income was received annually in arrears. In practice, it is received quarterly in advance and, although the tables have been modified, much traditional valuation uses the original assumption for simplicity. However, whatever income basis is used, the two essential elements required to perform the calculation are: the period of time the investment is to last in terms of years and the rate of return required, usually known as the all-risks yield (ARY).

   To summarise: in order to estimate the capital value of an interest in real property using the traditional investment method, three elements are required:

(i) the net income to be received;
(ii) the period for which the net income will be received;
(iii) the required yield.

(i) and (ii) will be obtained from the lease of the subject property or, if the property is unlet, an estimate of the rental value will be obtained from lettings of comparable properties. (iii) will be obtained from analysis of sales of comparable investments. A valuer must therefore have knowledge of two separate markets: the letting and the investment markets. Example 1.2 provides a basic investment method calculation.

Example 1.2: A basic investment method calculation

Assume prime shops in Oxford Street have a yield of 4 per cent. The income from the shop you are interested in is £200,000 net p.a. How much would you pay for the freehold interest?

Net income	£200,000 p.a.
Year's Purchase @ 4% in perpetuity	× 25 YP*
Capital value	£5,000,000

$$^*YP = \frac{100\%}{Yield} = \frac{100\%}{4\%} = 25\,YP$$

The valuation set out in the example has been set out below as a basic spreadsheet (Example 1.3) to show how the calculation can be done. The spreadsheet is best constructed as follows:

Set out the data to be used in the calculation

↓

Set out the text of the valuation before inserting values

↓

Insert values

Note that the cells C1 and C5 are formatted as percentages, so the number used by the spreadsheet will be the decimal equivalent, in this case 0.04. This is why the calculation in D5 uses 1/C5 rather than 100/C5.

Example 1.3: Spreadsheet version

	A	B	C	D	E	F
1	**Data:**	Yield	4.00%		**FORMULA USED**	
2		Income	200000			
3						
4		Net income		200000	= **C2**	
5		Year's purchase @	4.00%	25	= **1/C5**	
6		Capital value		5000000	= **D4*D5**	
7						

The investment method

In order to understand the basis of the traditional method and the use of compounding and discounting factors in investment calculations, we need to consider the tables that underpin the appraisals. In dealing with investment situations, we are considering the purchase of an asset to generate an income stream over a period of time; thus we are converting the value of an income stream in the future into a present capital sum. The basis of the traditional approach, the tables used in *Parry's Tables*, is about the conversion of present and future sums and the conversions of capital and income streams. The tables deal with the process of compounding and discounting, for instance the *Amount of £1* table will add compound interest to an initial sum to give a future capital sum. The six main options of conversion are:

- capital to income, and vice versa;
- present sums to future sums, and vice versa;
- the compounding of income flows into future capital sums and discounting back of future income flows to a present capital value.

A summary of the valuation tables and the explanation of their use is set out in Chapter 6.

SUMMARY OF CHAPTER

- This chapter has introduced the basic principles involved in property investment.
- It has examined different concepts of valuation and price in the market context.
- It has begun to look at applying these concepts in the calculations used in traditional property valuation.

REFERENCES AND BIBLIOGRAPHY

Barter, S. L. (1988) 'Introduction', in S. L. Barter (ed.), *Real Estate Finance*, Butterworths, London.

Brett, M. (1989) 'Characteristics of property', *Estates Gazette*, 21 January, p.14.

Brown, G. R. (1991) *Property Investment and the Capital Markets*, E. & F. N. Spon, London.

Darlow, C. (ed.) (1983) *Valuation and Investment Appraisal*, Estates Gazette, London.

Davidson, A. W. (1989) *Parry's Valuation and Investment Tables*, Estates Gazette, London.

Dubben, N. and Sayce, S. (1991) *Property Portfolio Management: An Introduction*, Routledge, London.

Fraser, W. D. (1993) *Principles of Property Investment and Pricing*, Macmillan – now Palgrave, London.

Isaac, D. and Steley, T. (2000) *Property Valuation Techniques*, Macmillan – now Palgrave, London.

Lennox, K. (1996) 'Thumbs up for property: IPF/EG survey', *Estates Gazette*, 20 April, p.41.

Pike, R. and Neale, B. (1993) *Corporate Finance and Investment*, Prentice Hall, London.

2 The Principles of Investment Applied to Property

2.1 The qualities of an investment
2.2 Characteristics of property as an investment
2.3 Property investment compared with other investments

AIMS AND OBJECTIVES

This chapter discusses the qualities of an investment. It analyses the characteristics of property investment and compares property with other competing investments.

2.1 THE QUALITIES OF AN INVESTMENT

The approach to the analysis of what is required of an investment is best done as a checklist of questions and answers. The major question is: What does an investor expect from the investment? The answers might be:

- security of capital and also liquidity so that the interest can be disposed of easily;
- security of income from the capital invested;
- regularity of income;
- low cost of purchase and sale of the investment;
- ease of purchase and sale of the investment;
- divisibility of the investment (am I able to sell off bits of it?);
- security in real terms (is the value of the investment increasing in line with inflation?);
- opportunities of growth in value (is it more or less than the rate of inflation, i.e. real growth or not?).

These qualities are summarised in Table 2.1, which compares the characteristics of a number of possible investment opportunities. Some investments out-perform others in this comparison but the characteristics of the investment types also involve start-up costs and security. The additional key

Table 2.1 The characteristics of investment compared with types of investment

Characteristics of investment	Type of investment					
	Vacant house	Tenanted house	Shares	Index linked government stock (ILG*)	Building society accounts	Premium bonds
Security of nominal capital	depends on the market	if tenants vacate, yes; otherwise depends	depends on company	yes	yes	yes
Security of income	no	no	depends on company	yes	yes	no
Regularity of income	no	yes	yes	yes	yes	no
Ease of purchase and sale	no	no	yes	yes	yes	yes
Low cost of purchase and sale	no	no	no	yes	yes	yes
Divisibility	no	no	yes	yes	yes	yes
Real security/growth (hedge against inflation)	depends	depends	depends	yes	no	no

* ILG = Index Linked Gilts.

variable is the size of return and whether this outstrips inflation, and this is considered in the final row of the table. The real security is considered here, once inflation has been allowed for, in the capital value and income of the investment; that is, whether the capital value has fallen in real value and whether the return is paying off inflation and more. Real values can be thought of in terms of purchasing power; if this declines in terms of capital value or income then the real value return is falling and the investment can be considered inflation-prone (as opposed to inflation-proof). The various elements which investors consider in their returns are discussed later in the chapter.

The type of investment chosen is related to a number of factors, and these will differ according to the investor. There may be a particular or peculiar arrangement; tax arrangements, for instance, or ethical considerations that may affect investment choice. The quality of an investment from an economic point of view must be a comparison of the return to the risk; the return is not just the cash flow arising but this needs to be considered in relation to the original outlay and return on possible sale. So the cash flow needs to be considered relative to the original outlay, ongoing costs, and risks involved in future income and capital revenues. A more detailed analysis would look at three prime areas: economic influences, psychic influences and aspects relating to social responsibility. The major influence is the economic one and this relates to the risk/return profile of the investment. There are a number of aspects relating to risk and return of capital, and income and the associated area of external injections and taxation of income and capital, these matters being essentially financial considerations. Other aspects which affect the risk and return are time matters relating to the incidence of in- and out-flows of income and capital; the life of the asset is associated with this, as is the concept of depreciation in value of the asset. Finally, risk and return are related to the liquidity of the asset and problems of management.

2.2 CHARACTERISTICS OF PROPERTY AS AN INVESTMENT

An investment is an asset which produces income or capital growth that will convert to income during or at the end of the life of the asset. The investment market is often considered peculiar to the UK, a situation where investors in property construct buildings which others occupy and pay rent. Such a situation may be a product of the development of the landed estates, where historically the landed gentry as a class were divorced from those organising and engaged in manufacturing and commerce. Such a debate is beyond the objectives of this book but certainly the landlord/tenant relationship on such a wide scale appears peculiar to the UK and some countries of the old Commonwealth (even in the previously British territory of Hong Kong, the land was generally owned by the government). This is not to say that there is little owner occupation in the UK but considerations of space allocation here relate more to economic factors such as production, labour and profit rather than to investment returns arising from property and land.

Darlow (1983) has suggested three major reasons for this situation:

(i) a high percentage of the savings of individuals (the collectivisation of savings, discussed elsewhere in this book) is channelled through a small number of private-sector financial institutions which have to find investment for their resulting cash flows;
(ii) the tendency among many manufacturers and retailers in the UK is to rent rather than own the properties they occupy, thus creating an income-producing investment for a potential landlord;
(iii) the planning climate in the UK has for most of the post-war period kept the supply of good-quality commercial property below demand. Thus rents have offered protection against inflation, because of shortages, and capital values have appreciated.

Principles of property investment

As an introduction to property investment it is useful to make comparisons with, for instance, investment in shares. Such a comparison is often applied to the respective returns but the mechanism and structure of investment in the two media is radically different. These initial differences were summarised by Brett (1989) and are shown in the Box 2.1.

Property valuation is a means of providing an assessment of the capital value of, or the income arising from, a property investment. There is a range of possible investment opportunities from works of art through oil futures and gold to shares, government stocks and property. The point of investment is that it provides the investor with an income, growth in capital value of the investment, or both.

Property investment is a long-term commitment of funds. Transfer costs and purchase time (up to six months) restrict opportunities for short-term dealings. Investors in property are looking for growth of income and capital. Note that these two aspects are interrelated through the relationship of the all-risks yield = income/capital value. In the UK the tradition in the commercial market is for occupiers to lease premises, thus ownership and occupation are split and an investment market in property is opened up. In the USA and Europe there is more owner occupation. In considering the characteristics of property investment it is necessary to look at a number

**BOX 2.1: THE CHARACTERISTICS OF PROPERTY:
A COMPARISON WITH COMPANY SHARES
(adapted from Brett, 1989)**

1. Commercial properties are of high value, whereas shares can be broken down to smaller sizes of ownership. Property ownership thus tends to be in the hands of large financial institutions rather than individuals.
2. Property is not a standardised investment; one share in a particular company is the same as another but properties are not identical.
3. Property is not a pre-packaged investment, whereas with a share you buy the management. With property, you will need to manage it yourself or pay someone to do it for you.
4. Property is an investment that can be improved by active management. You cannot do this with shares. Property investment may require additional new money to restructure leases, to refurbish or to redevelop buildings, however.
5. Property investment can be created by finding sites, erecting buildings and finding tenants.
6. Points 3–5 show that some expertise is required in investing in and managing property.
7. There is no single market for commercial property; it is a localised market. The time spent in buying and selling is greater than that with shares.
8. Market information is often imperfect and the data surrounding transactions are often not available or kept confidential.
9. The income stream from property is often geared to rent reviews in leases, and income increases will not be available until the next review, whereas the income stream from share dividends may change half yearly.
10. Property investment can literally wear out (depreciation of buildings) or be made worthless by activities (as with land contamination).
11. There are a variety of ownerships in land, from freeholds to leases and licences that affect the value of the interest and the level and risk of income arising.
12. Different property interests will be of interest to different types of investor depending on their tax status or investment requirements for income, capital growth or risk avoidance.
13. Different types of property (different sectors such as retail, industrial and offices) generate different returns and have different risk profiles, and so may be chosen by differing investors.
14. Properties also have various risk profiles depending on whether they are prime (best quality), secondary or tertiary.
15. Property is presented as a long-term investment but may not necessarily be so. Most owners do, however, retain their properties for long periods of time.

of factors: the property investment market, the nature of income, the rate
of return and the level of income.

The nature of the market

The market is fragmented and poorly recorded, and there is no central focus
for trading either through a central market or via a computerised screen.
Property is diverse and each property has unique characteristics, so the
market is unstructured. The locational characteristics can reduce the size of
the market. There is imperfect knowledge in the market (hence the difference between valuation, price and worth). There are no central prices or
registry of transactions, as land registry files have only recently been made
available to the public. There is restriction of movement into and out of the
market because of the constraints of time, legal considerations and financial considerations, so prices stick. In the short run the supply of property
is inelastic. This can be seen from Figure 2.1 showing economic supply and
demand: the supply S is fixed and if demand is increased from D_1 to D_2
then the price increases from P_1 to P_2, more than if the supply was elastic
(then the S curve would be upward sloping).

Nature of the income

The market is made up of a number of types of investment, which produce
different types of income; for instance: rack rented freeholds, reversionary
investments, secure ground rents, short leasehold profit rents, turnover rents

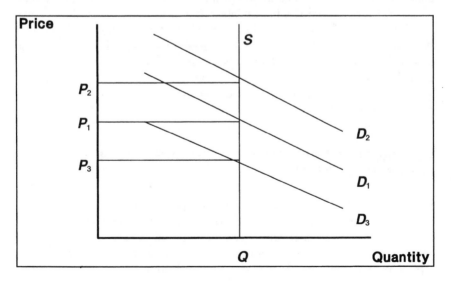

Figure 2.1 *Supply of land*

and so on. The type of investment will determine the amount and timing of the income stream.

The rate of return

The rate of return can be analysed in its simplified form from an analysis of initial (all-risk) yields. An analysis of yield levels over the last 25 years shows that for prime yields (little research has been carried out in areas other than for prime properties) there is less variation than in other investment indices. Since 1977, when the investment market was becoming more settled after the crash of 1974, property yields provided a more stable performance than indices relating to gilt yields or the level of interest rates.

Level of income

Changes in the level of rental value over time show a relationship with the level of inflation. Thus although the money level of rents has varied over the period, the real level of rents shows a real increase, especially during periods of high inflation. In respect of property as an investment, land is more durable than other commodities. Purchasers buy land for future income or use, thus they forego present consumption to do this. If purchasers buy property for occupation by themselves, they are in the position of receiving an income equivalent to a rent that they would otherwise have to pay if they did not own the property. Property is thus purchased for investment as well as consumption. Land is heterogeneous as each piece is different. Each property is unique by location but properties do have some characteristics in common and one property can be substituted for another.

The price of property is high relative to individual earnings, thus people borrow to buy property and the availability of credit has an important bearing on demand. Legal factors have a serious effect on the supply and demand for property; the Rent Acts which controlled income from residential tenanted property, for instance, restricted the rights to increase the level of rents and thus led to a subsequent decline in investment in the private rented sector.

2.3 PROPERTY INVESTMENT COMPARED WITH OTHER INVESTMENTS

Property is only one of a number of competing investment media, and investors will put together a portfolio of different investments to reflect their attitudes to risk and return and perhaps other objectives (social and psychological as well as economic, as previously discussed). In 1989 a typical institutional portfolio (pension fund or insurance company) would be UK equities (55 per cent), overseas equities (22 per cent), gilts (12 per cent), property (8 per cent) and cash and other investments (2 per cent) (Dubben and Sayce, 1991). This ratio of holdings has varied greatly over a number of years, with the property proportion rising to 25 per cent at its peak and falling to around 7 per cent by 1996; this falling-off in the allocation of property in institutional funds' portfolios is of great concern to the property profession. Sweeney (1988) has suggested, using a mean-variance technique, that the inclusion of property in the portfolio reduces risk and that low-risk portfolios should have at least 20 per cent property content.

Beside property as an investment, there are a number of alternatives:

Bank and building society accounts
Articles for use (chattels)
National savings
Guaranteed income and growth bonds
Government and public authority shares
Company stocks and shares
Unit trusts and investment trusts
Futures and traded options

To obtain a balanced portfolio, an investor will want a spread of investments similar to the way a unit trust works, but investors will usually choose a mixture of government stocks (gilts) and company shares as the basis for a portfolio.

SUMMARY OF CHAPTER

- This chapter has examined investment qualities in general and then focused on property.
- It has looked at the specific investment characteristics of property.
- It has compared property with other types of investment.

REFERENCES AND BIBLIOGRAPHY

Balchin, P. N., Isaac, D. and Chen, J. (2000) *Urban Economics: A Global Perspective*, Palgrave, Basingstoke, Hants/New York.
Brett, M. (1989) 'Characteristics of property', *Estates Gazette*, 21 January, p.14.
Darlow, C. (ed.) (1983) *Valuation and Investment Appraisal*, Estates Gazette, London.
Dubben, N. and Sayce, S. (1991) *Property Portfolio Management: An Introduction*, Routledge, London.
Sweeney, F. (1988) '20% in property – a viable strategy', *Estates Gazette*, 13 February, pp.26–8.

3 The Property Market

3.1 The property market
3.2 What affects property values?
3.3 Legal aspects
3.4 Investment in property

AIMS AND OBJECTIVES

This chapter examines the factors which influence property values and goes on to consider:

- legal interests in land;
- legislation affecting land and buildings.

Key terms

Open market value – the best price at which an interest in a property might reasonably be expected to be sold by private treaty at the date of valuation.
Freeholds – properties in which the owners hold ownership absolutely and in perpetuity.
Leaseholds – properties that are subject to legal agreements allowing the lessees rights over the property for a term of years.

3.1 THE PROPERTY MARKET

Owner–occupier and investment markets

Property development is the process by which buildings are erected for occupation or for sale/investment. Owners may build premises for their own occupation, for example major retailers may erect supermarkets; alternatively, property developers may construct the same type of buildings for lease or sale. The process may be the same in both cases, although some aspects of the financial appraisal may be different. A building offered for sale or investment is driven by a profit motive, while a building for owner occupation may be related to the profitability of the enterprise within the building and thus profit motivation may be constrained. Property investment and development are much like any other economic activity, satisfying wants through the application of scarce resources. In the case of property, the wants are for space to work in, sell from, live in and enjoy recreational activities in. The process by which buildings are erected to provide space employs the key factors of production: land for the site, capital for purchase of the land and materials, and labour to erect a building. In addition there is the need to manage the process, and the entrepreneurial talent of the property developer to initiate the process and bring the pieces together.

The owner–occupier sector has tended to be overlooked in property texts, except for those of a macro-economic nature. The problem lies in the fact that there is a substantial investment market in the UK where properties are developed for lease and sale, and it is this activity that is the most traditional approach for property developers in the property markets. This is unlike the situation in continental European markets where development is more likely to be for the purpose of owner occupation.

Owner occupation is also much more important in emerging economies and in economies in transitions from non-market forms. Analysis of the development of property investment markets in Eastern Europe, for instance, provides a clear indication that owner–occupiers give a kick-start to development and investment markets, especially where they are outside companies or individual investors. In Hungary, the Czech Republic and Poland there is evidence that as economies have opened up from state control, so outside operators have wanted to establish plants. The investment market initially was non-existent, as was local finance for any projects. These are two of the necessary precursors for the development of property markets and, interestingly, often the two elements that are missing in emerging economies or economies in transition from a command to a market economy. China is another example of this problem. What happens in these situations is that the foreign company usually sets up a partnership arrangement with local producers, for instance a joint venture. The difficulty then is that there are no suitable premises available, so the foreign company builds its own (in these cases, the outside company acts as a developer and kick-starts the development market). In addition, as local finance is not forthcoming, the foreign company needs to obtain this from its home market or international sources. This leads to an injection of external capital, thus stimulating the local financial market. As the company expands and requires more or different premises, so it buys and sells buildings, thus stimulating the investment market, especially where it has to retain old premises for re-letting as there are few owner–occupiers with capital to purchase. Success of such operations can then encourage further real estate activity; for instance, profit from land sales may, in a rapidly improving market, prove to be a more important contribution to profit than sales of the product, especially if the economy is emerging slowly. The role of the foreign company thus could be influential in the development, investment and financial sectors, and the other interesting factor could be that foreign agents arrive to ensure the system starts to work properly. Evidence from Eastern European countries mentioned previously suggests that while German, French and Italian companies may be taking the lead in investment and finance, UK firms dominate the agency business (Balchin *et al.*, 2000).

A final point, which applies both to emerging and to established economies, is the nature of finance. In periods of boom and slump in property markets, finance can have a major effect. If money is easy to come by at cheap rates, this can have an effect on development and investment activity and can lead to inflation of prices and a boom situation. The property boom of the late 1980s in the UK was fuelled by bank finance mainly from overseas and foreign banks. The bubble in the Japanese economy in the late 1980s was also fuelled by easy bank finance. A scheme referred to by some as 'property pin-ball' suggested that banks generated the inflation in values by constantly arranging for the buying and selling of the same property with appropriate increases in value. The banks benefited from the fees on the transactions but also provided the inflated valuations so that the process could carry on until the bubble burst, leading to the collapse of the property market and three major banks becoming insolvent.

The property market is sometimes held to be inefficient; if this is so then actual prices and values will differ. Research in the UK has suggested that overall the market may not be inefficient and that market knowledge is reflected in the prices, so values will be close to actual prices (Brown, 1991). Traditionally though, in most sectors of the market, the view has been taken that the market is inefficient. There are a number of reasons for inefficiency:

- lack of data on market transactions;
- lack of homogeneity in property assets – they are all different and thus difficult to value;
- lack of liquidity in the market.

Lack of liquidity in the property market

This is specifically due to a number of conditions in the market, namely:

- high transaction and entry costs to the market, lotting problems (properties are sold in expensive lot sizes), the size of lots and their indivisibility;
- lack of transactions, meaning that valuation is difficult;

- lack of a market infrastructure, so transactions are slow to complete;
- lack of a central marketplace, only localised markets being available;
- legal problems in the nature of registering land and ensuring the registers contain any debts against the asset and the proof of title.

3.2 WHAT AFFECTS PROPERTY VALUES?

- The international situation can affect levels of confidence in the market but probably not as badly as in the stock market. Interest rates will affect borrowing and therefore activity in the new and second-hand markets for property, that is the development of new property as well as investment in existing property.
- The mood of the national economy affects the confidence of investors. The levels of disposable income available affect house prices and the amount available for investment.
- Government policies affect property values. Property is taxed both in terms of capital gains and the income derived from rents. Changes in the tax situation can affect the investor's interest. Also government legislation can encourage or discourage investment directly or through its fiscal (tax) and monetary (adjustment of interest rates) policy.
- The local economy can affect land prices. Land prices and rents will tend to be higher in areas where the local economy is thriving. This could be shown in the comparison in the 1980s between house prices and industrial rentals in the London suburbs and, say, the north-east of England.
- Geography and location are also important for value. Geography is important in terms of value, and the geology, topography and climate give rise to the most fertile and thus the most expensive agricultural land (in the UK this is located in eastern England). Location is important, and office blocks may need to be close to a business area, have transport links and have reasonable surroundings.
- Fashion and local demand can affect price. Trendy areas and locations can increase price levels, as can the gentrification of traditional working-class areas. Favoured locations may be the spin-off of successful regeneration opportunities, such as Covent Garden in London or in areas of historical or interesting built environments like Greenwich.
- The individual design features of properties can affect value. These may include architectural details, the space and design, the scale and nature of the garden, and the age and style of the property.
- Tenure may affect the property price; a property may be freehold or leasehold. This is an important area of valuation and is discussed later.
- Condition and state of repair will affect value, as will the availability of services. The services include the provision of central heating in a house

and the installation of air conditioning or computer wiring/trunking in an office building.

- The potential for extension, renovation, reuse and redevelopment will affect the value.
- The ease of purchase and sale, that is the ease of transferability, will also affect the property price. Prices will be depressed if the transaction takes a long time to complete. Property investors are often paying interest on monies used for purchase. Lack of information can also affect property prices. Because of the nature of the investment, people will not generally buy a property investment unless they have full details of the investment. You would not buy a property, for instance, unless you had carried out the necessary searches of the title and investigated any future developments that may affect the property.

The factors affecting property values are summarised in Figure 3.1.

Impacts on property values can be psychological and social rather than economic. The owner of a large historic house may view the ownership to be very prestigious or else may be concerned about the social responsibility of its upkeep and maintenance.

Odd things can affect property values; one example, for instance, is *feng sui*. This is an oriental art concerned with the orientation of buildings and space that includes the juxtaposition of rooms within buildings and objects within the internal space, as well as the external orientation. *The Times* suggested that, in the late 1990s in the UK, the property boom had been paralleled by a boom in *feng sui* consultancy for prospective house pur-

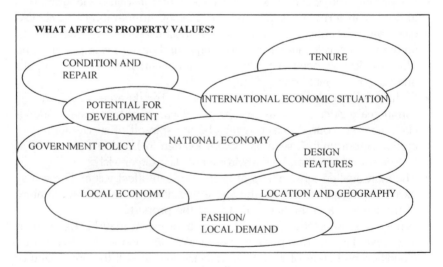

WHAT AFFECTS PROPERTY VALUES?

CONDITION AND REPAIR

TENURE

POTENTIAL FOR DEVELOPMENT

INTERNATIONAL ECONOMIC SITUATION

GOVERNMENT POLICY

NATIONAL ECONOMY

DESIGN FEATURES

LOCAL ECONOMY

LOCATION AND GEOGRAPHY

FASHION/ LOCAL DEMAND

Figure 3.1 *What affects property values?*

chasers. An example is quoted of the frustrated purchase of a stone-built cottage in Yorkshire that faced a main road and a stone wall. The *feng sui* report suggested that positive energies were being 'whisked away' and blocked at the same time because of the position of the house. The report suggested that such a location would give 'little support in moving toward the future'. *The Times* quotes the chairman of the Feng Sui Society in the UK as defining *feng sui* as a 'complex art involving disciplines from site planning to psychology that explain how the environment affects our lives'.

3.3 LEGAL ASPECTS

The two principal interests in land are freehold and leasehold interests. Other legal interests or estates in land are easements, restrictive covenants and licences. Freeholds are properties in which the owners hold ownership absolutely and in perpetuity. The owner is either in possession of the property (i.e. the occupier) or derives rents arising from leases or tenancies granted (an investor). Leasehold properties are subject to legal agreements allowing the lessees rights over the property for a term of years. Freehold and leasehold interests are defined as 'legal estates' by the Law of Property Act 1925 and these are enforceable against anyone. Other interests are termed equitable interests and can be enforced against some people only. Leasehold and equitable interests are carved out of the freehold interest. At the end of a lease there is a reversion to the landlord (that is, the property ownership reverts back to him). However, this reversion has been restricted by government legislation, for instance the Rents Act affected short leases and the Leasehold Reform Act affected long leases, the Agricultural Holdings Act affected agricultural land, and the Landlord and Tenant Act affected commercial property. There are two principal types of lease:

- The *building* or *ground lease*, where the lessee (the person who takes the lease) erects buildings on the vacant site. These leases tend to be long leases because of the obligation to build, and are usually 99 or 125 years but could be as much as 999 years.
- The *occupation lease*, where the lease is of both land and buildings for occupation. The lease is a medium- to long-term one, perhaps 20 or 25 years, with the rent being reviewed every 5 years.

Sub-leases are granted by lessees and carved from their leasehold interest. The nature of leases and sub-leases is shown in Figure 3.2.

Other interests include restrictive covenants and easements that are restrictions on the use of land by a freeholder or leaseholder. A covenant is a contractual obligation in a deed. An easement is a right under common law that burdens one piece of land for the benefit of another. Easements

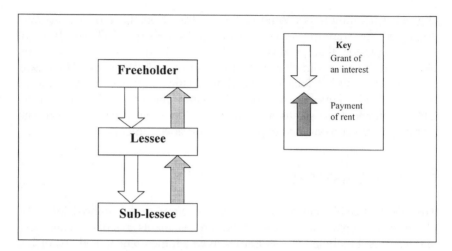

Figure 3.2 *The granting of legal interests*

Table 3.1 *Legal and equitable interests*

Legal interests	Equitable interests
Legal interests and legal estates, that is: <ul><li>freeholds</li><li>leaseholds</li><li>easements</li><li>covenants</li></ul>	*Equitable interests, grants under wills or settlements, that is:* <ul><li>permissions to enter land</li><li>licences</li></ul>

are such things as rights of way, rights of support, and rights of light and ventilation. Interests in land have to be distinguished from permission to enter upon land, such as licences, and the differences are shown in Table 3.1.

Legislation on land and premises

Besides the legal interests involved in land, land is also constrained by government statutes. As has been described earlier, the government can intervene in respect of lessees and tenants of certain properties, both to give security of tenure and to control levels of rent. The government also intervenes through its fiscal policy to tax income and capital gains arising from land. Finally, local authorities have statutory control over the development and use of land through the Town and Country Planning Acts and over the construction of buildings through the Building Regulations. There is a myriad of legislation relating to the use and condition of premises, including the Offices, Shops and Railway Premises Act, the Factories Act, the Fire Precautions Act, the Housing Acts, and Health and Safety legislation.

3.4 INVESTMENT IN PROPERTY

Property plays an important part in investment and commerce both as an investment in its own right and as a security for various forms of lending. For the individual investor, shares in a quoted property company are usually the most attractive way of investing in commercial property. The traditional property investment company has a number of characteristics that differentiate it from firms in the manufacturing or service sectors. Usually, it shows a relatively low current yield and the shares are bought mainly for long-term capital and income growth. The property company may finance itself to a greater extent on borrowed money than most manufacturing concerns and it is likely to pay out a higher proportion of its earnings by way of dividend.

Though the property companies' shares will be valued partly according to their yield, the asset backing is also important. Thus it is not just profitability but the asset base on which the profits are generated (from rents or disposals) which is important. If the liabilities of the company are deducted from the value of the properties and any other assets it owns, the resultant sum is what belongs to the shareholders. This sum, divided by the number of shares, gives a figure for the net asset value per share. The market value of the shares will normally stand somewhat below this figure and this is referred to as a *discount to net asset value*. Shares in a property company are described as giving a yield of so much per cent, and standing at a discount of say 30 per cent to net assets. This does not mean that the company necessarily has any intention of selling its properties, or that the shareholders would necessarily receive as much as the net asset value for the shares if it did, as capital gains tax on disposal of the properties might have to be paid. Rather, this approach is more of a yardstick for comparing the assets of one company with another and can also serve as indicator of income growth in the future (which is presumed to be based on the income-generating ability of the assets). The relationship between share price and net asset value can fluctuate within wide limits and in the analysis it is important to distinguish between property investment and trading companies. Property investment companies obtain their income from rents; trading companies obtain their income from sale of completed developments. The idea of a *development* company, on the other hand, is not a useful concept, as it does not help in distinguishing the two principal objectives of the company to develop either for investment or for trade. The major developers, in terms of the scale of development activity, will tend to be the investment companies rather than the trading companies, although development activity may be carried out by a separate subsidiary.

The majority of quoted property companies invest mainly in commercial and industrial property, in other words in office buildings, shops, warehouses and factories. Residential property has become increasing unpopular as an income-yielding investment because of rent controls and other restrictions imposed by successive governments. Most property companies will have a fair mix of different types of commercial property, though some will tend to specialise in one type: shops (as a name applies) in the case of Capital Shopping, or factory and warehouse buildings in the case of Slough Estates. Companies may also specialise by geographical area. The biggest of them all, Land Securities Investment Trust, has a spread of different types of top-quality commercial and industrial property throughout the UK but is probably best known for its portfolio of office properties in Central London.

Some companies hold a fair proportion of their properties overseas, particularly in Continental Europe with some investment in North America. Often, however, these overseas ventures have met with disappointing returns and the US market is a particularly specialist and difficult area to operate in. Property companies differ not only by geographical location and by the type of property they own, but the nature of the operation they undertake will also differ. The commercial property investment company, to which we have referred earlier, does much of what its name suggests: it owns properties and sees its income and the value of its assets rise as inflation and shortages of space force rent upwards in a good market. Many reaped, during the 1980s, the rewards from properties constructed twenty years before. If the income of the property company comes entirely from rents from well-located companies, this income is of very high quality. Up to the end of the 1980s, the rental income could be predicted to a degree but since then rental values have fallen and the incidence of over-renting is now very apparent. It is therefore far more difficult to assess the expectations of rental income at the next rent review. The forecasting of future cash flow streams to the investment has thus also become very difficult.

Property investment involves a long-term investment and a commitment because of the nature of the returns and the costs of transferability. Many property investors are also property developers but the latter may well keep property developments in their portfolio rather than dispose of them, as property traders would do. Well-selected properties can offer income growth and capital growth over the longer period. Property investment in the UK is strong because of the nature of the investment market, with occupiers taking leases for occupation rather than buying themselves. In many European countries, for instance, this would not be the norm and owner occupation would predominate. The main considerations for investment are:

- the nature of the legal interest being acquired;
- the location of the investment and surrounding environment;
- the nature and design of the property itself;
- planning proposals for the area;
- the terms of existing leases;
- expectation of income and capital growth from the property investment;
- the level of future demand, both for renting the accommodation and selling the investment at some future date;
- possible future changes in fashion, technology, demography and transportation infrastructure;
- underlying national economic trends;
- structural changes within the industry or sector from where tenant demand originates;
- current and future level of available competitive accommodation;
- government intervention, new legislation and taxes (Darlow, 1983).

The acquisition sequence

The process of purchase of a property asset is complex and the sequence of acquisition is shown in Figure 3.3. This outlines the details of the procedures carried out in the acquisition process.

Exercise question

There are a number of factors which can affect property values and which property investors should consider. Discuss the main factors.

Outline answer

You need to reflect on a range of factors that may have effect on property values. These factors could include:

General features:
The international finance markets
The national economic situation
Existing supply of this type of property
Government policy and incentives
The local economy
The geographical location – latitude, topography, aspect and climate
Fashion and local demand.

Continued

The individual features of a property:
State of repair
Costs-in-use
Services
Technological design and fittings
Development potential, and time period to complete development.

You should be able to give examples of the effect of each factor on values.

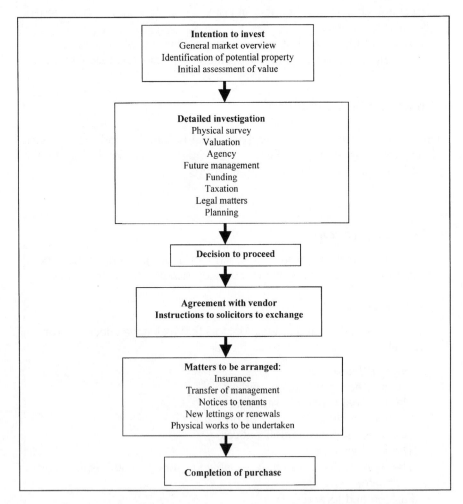

Figure 3.3 *Acquisition sequence [adapted from Darlow, 1983]*

SUMMARY OF CHAPTER

This chapter has examined property markets, including:
- The nature of the property market and liquidity in the market.
- Factors affecting the property market.
- The investment market in property.
- Legal aspects and the acquisition sequence.

REFERENCES AND BIBLIOGRAPHY

Balchin, P. N., Isaac, D. and Chen, J. (2000) *Urban Economics: A Global Perspective*, Palgrave, Basingstoke, Hants/New York.

Brown, G. R. (1991) *Property Investment and the Capital Markets*, E. & F. N. Spon, London.

Darlow, C. (ed.) (1983) *Valuation and Investment Appraisal*, Estates Gazette, London.

4 The Role of the Valuer

4.1 The process of valuation
4.2 Types of valuation
4.3 Market valuation and the 'Red Book'
4.4 Sources of information for the valuer on the Web

AIMS AND OBJECTIVES

This chapter examines the process of valuation and introduces the basic methods. It distinguishes the different types of valuation, especially open market valuation. It concludes with an overview of the *Valuation and Appraisal Manual* of the Royal Institution of Chartered Surveyors.

Key terms

Appraisal – includes property valuation and investment analysis.
Property valuation – the estimation of market price.
Investment analysis – the analysis of worth.

4.1 THE PROCESS OF VALUATION

Valuation is a matter of opinion; it is an individual's subjective assessment of different factors. Different weights can be given to various opinions, and a valuer who has studied the different methods of valuation and who gets his/her valuations to accord with market evidence will be listened to and inform others. Computers can assist with the assembling of market evidence and comparable transactions, and they can be used for complex mathematical calculations, but in the end, however, it is the art of valuation that counts. A valuer is required to value property, which is to find a market value when the market transaction for the property has yet to take place. This is a responsible decision and expensive if things go wrong; if you put a property up for sale at too low a valuation you are likely to lose money, at too high a valuation the property will stick on the market and take a long time to sell if at all.

To clarify the valuation approach, it is important to distinguish between property appraisal, market valuation and investment analysis. Recent debates have combined with criticism of traditional approaches of property valuation over the last 20 years or so to demand that, in the area which has previously been termed property valuation, more extensive analysis be provided. Generally the approach that should be taken (Baum and Crosby, 1995) is that the overall property appraisal should be clearly divided between property valuation for purchase (valuation for market price) and the subsequent analysis of performance. In the first case this is defined as *valuation* and in the second case it is defined as *analysis*; the overall process is termed *property appraisal*. Thus the valuation of a property (the calculation of the exchange value of property) is different from the subsequent analysis of the performance of the property as an investment (the appraisal of its actual worth). Calculations before and after purchase will not agree because of the lack of perfect knowledge in the market at the time of the transaction and the inability to predict future changes in the cash flow and the risk profile of the investment accurately. Thus the techniques discussed later on in this book can be used to anticipate the market value or else to record and analyse the progress of the investment subsequent to purchase. It is critical to understand the difference between these two approaches in the property appraisal process.

Having considered the above, the traditional methods used in valuation are called the five methods, these are:

- the investment method;
- the comparative method;
- the contractor's method (a cost-based method);
- the profits method; and
- the residual valuation.

The *residual* valuation is used in development situations but may also rely heavily on the other methods. It may use the investment method, for instance, to determine the gross development value of the proposed development, or it may use the comparative method to compare capital values or site values calculated with examples from the market. The costs calculated for building works are a form of the contractor's method. Depending on the type of property, the profits method may also be used to determine the gross development value. A final point to be made about the valuation of the site, which is the outcome of the residual valuation, is that the value of land is determined by its use and the intensity of use. Land may have development potential but it will require planning permission for any form of development except for some minor works and some changes of use.

The Town and Country Planning Acts determine this process of granting permission to develop. The Town and Country Planning Act 1990 basically defines *development* as:

> *the carrying out of building and other operations on, under or over land.*

4.2 TYPES OF VALUATION

The two main types of valuation are statutory and non-statutory valuations. Statutory valuations are for purposes for which there are rules laid down by law. The main types of statutory valuation are:

- *Valuation for rating*: Here the District Valuer, who is employed by the Inland Revenue, assesses the property to Gross Value or Net Annual Value. Properties other than specialised buildings or industrial buildings are assessed to Gross Value (GV), from which certain deductions are made to Rateable Value (RV). The RV × rate in the £1 charged by the local authority = rates to be paid. The GV is an assessment of the rental value of the premises at the time the rating list was drawn up.
- *Valuation for compulsory purchase*: This is based on the compensation payable under statute and case law.
- *Valuation for tax*: For instance, capital gains tax on property assets.
- *Assessments for fair rents*: For rented dwellings.

Statutory valuations are based on market valuations but there are assumptions that are frequently made in the valuation. Compensation for compulsory purchase, for instance, ignores the scheme of development for which the purchase is made.

Examples of non-statutory valuations are:

- *Valuations for buying and selling property*: Here the valuation can be shown to be correct by the actual price achieved in the market.
- *Valuations for rental*: On letting a property or taking a lease or tenancy.
- *Valuations for fire insurance*: Based on the cost of reinstatement, that is the cost of rebuilding the property.
- *Mortgage valuation*: Where a loan or mortgage is being granted to buy the property or where the property is being used as security for another transaction.
- *Valuation for company accounts*.

A summary of the types of valuation is shown in Figure 4.1.

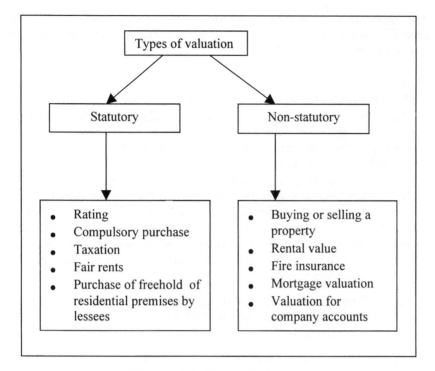

Figure 4.1   *Types of valuation*

Open market value

Open market value in the UK is basically:

> the best price at which an interest in a property might reasonably
> be expected to be sold by private treaty at the date of valuation,
> assuming:
>
> a) a willing seller (same as compulsory purchase assumptions);
> b) a reasonable period within which to negotiate, taking into account
>   the nature of the property and the state of the market;
> c) that values remain static through the period in b);
> d) the property will be freely exposed to the market (i.e. marketed
>   and advertised);
> e) no account be taken of any additional bid by a special purchase
>   (e.g. neighbour's bid).   [RICS, 1992]

The application of valuation methodology requires the definitions to be clear. The distinction between market price, valuation and worth must be clarified in this context.

Definitions

- *Market price* is the recorded consideration paid for a property.
- *Valuation* is the estimate of the most likely selling price, the assessment of which is the most common objective of the valuer. This 'most likely selling price' is commonly termed 'open market value' in the UK but is different from the concept of worth.
- *Worth* is the underlying investment value and consists of two aspects. Firstly, *individual worth* is the maximum bid price of an individual purchaser. Such a bid would take into account the appropriate use of all available data relating to the individual, the property and the market. Secondly, *market worth* is the price at which an investment would trade on a market where buyers and sellers were using all available information in an efficient manner.

The RICS (Royal Institution of Chartered Surveyors) *Appraisal and Valuation Manual* (the 'Red Book') (RICS, 1995) uses a number of definitions in this context including:

- *Appraisal*: The written provision of a valuation, combined with professional opinion or advice on the suitability of the subject property for a defined purpose.
- *Estimation of worth*: The provision of a written estimate of the net monetary worth of the subject property to the client.
- *Valuation*: The provision of a written opinion as to the price or value of the subject property on any given basis. It is specifically not a forecast.
- *Forecast*: The prediction of the likely value on a stated basis at a future specified date.

These valuation bases are agreed with the client prior to the valuation and should be appropriate to the client's needs but cannot override statutory definitions.

Asset valuation

Valuers are required to produce valuations for company purposes. These purposes are firstly, for asset values to be incorporated in the financial accounts of the company. Under the Companies Act, the company must produce, at the end of the accounting year, a balance sheet, a profit and loss account and a Directors' report. Secondly, the valuer can be required to value a company's assets for incorporation into a prospectus when a company is going public, that is selling shares to the public. This is a rule of admission of the company to the Stock Exchange, through which the public flotation takes place. Thirdly, the valuer can be required to value a company when subject to a take-over bid. Finally, to value assets for property bonds and trusts and general investment purposes.

Up until 1974 there were no guidelines on these valuations but in 1974 the RICS set up the Asset Valuation Standards Committee and in 1976 it issued its *Asset Valuation Guidance Notes*. The *Asset Valuation Guidance Notes* rejected the use of a going concern valuation. This is the idea that the assets of the company are more valuable to the company as a going concern than in the open market, because of the elements of goodwill that are attached to the assets. The basis of valuation is thus open market value (see Guidance Note A2). Open market value as defined in Guidance Note D1 has been set out earlier (RICS, 1992).

The definitions of open market value have been revised in the new 'Red Book' issued by the RICS (1995) and this will be discussed later in the chapter. Practice Statement P5 of the RICS' guidelines concern valuation for company accounts and financial statements. The Accounting Standards Board advocates the use of a 'value to the business' model in determining values in the balance sheet. Value to the business of an asset is the lower of its net current replacement cost and its recoverable amount. The recoverable amount is the higher of 'value in use' and 'net realisable value'. The net current replacement cost is the cost of purchasing, at the least cost, the remaining service potential of the asset at the balance sheet date. Value in use is the maximum amount recoverable from continuing ownership and ultimate disposal of the asset. Net realisable value is the estimated proceeds of sale of an asset less the selling cost. Continuing enterprises would normally have their assets valued to net current replacement cost (RICS, 1995). So:

- value to business = lower of net current replacement cost or recoverable amount;
- recoverable amount = higher of value in use or net realisable value.

4.3 MARKET VALUATION AND THE 'RED BOOK'

A revised definition of market value came into effect from 1 June 1992; the principal change is that the 'reasonable period' for marketing the interest is now assumed to have taken place before the valuation date. The valuation date in turn is assumed to coincide with the date of completion of the sale. To meet the point that, in practice, a purchase price is usually fixed not on the date of completion of the sale, but on an earlier date when unconditional contracts were exchanged, the valuer is required to assume that circumstances, values and market conditions at the date of contract were the same as those prevailing at the date of completion (i.e. the date of valuation). Thus there can no longer be an assumed marketing period following the date of valuation and so the provision that 'values will remain static' disappears. The 'reasonable period' in normal circumstances should not exceed a few months. The sale of an interest is assumed to have been completed unconditionally for a cash consideration. The valuer may not assume deferred completion, stage payments or consideration in terms of shares or an exchange of land. 'Proper marketing' means the most appropriate method to effect a disposal at the best price.

There has been some debate recently over the role of the mortgage valuation. It is generally accepted by the RICS guidance notes for valuers that the valuer should not make a recommendation as to the amount or the percentage of mortgage advance or as to the length of the mortgage term. The mortgage valuation has been the subject of debate in two areas. Firstly, in new house valuation where new house premiums may be taken into account. The premium relates to the fact that, as soon as the property is sold second-hand, there is likely to be a discount. A solution has been suggested that the valuations be carried out on the basis of a new house with the premium, provided it is stated that on immediate resale, the value will be reduced by a certain amount. The second debate on mortgage valuation relates to whether a warning should be given to the lender when valuing in a falling market. This would be especially important when valuing a property in the process of construction when only a small amount of building work had been carried out.

Recent criticisms and court cases reflecting the alleged negligence of professional valuers has led to some reconsideration of the advice given to purchasers. The problem may, of course, relate to a decline in the market whereby mistakes related to the calculation of market value at the time of transaction are not upheld by subsequent evidence. The Mallinson Report commissioned by the RICS and properly called the President's Working Party on Commercial Property Valuations reported in March 1994 (RICS, 1994). The Chairman suggested that there were four key areas that are described as needs or requirements of the valuer undertaking commercial property valuations. These needs are:

(i) Valuers need to be able to demonstrate to clients that, although there are many valuers who would make different judgements, all work is within a common body of knowledge, application and expression. Differences will therefore be as narrow as possible, and where they occur they will be reasonable and explicable, not perverse or chaotic.

(ii) Valuers need to demonstrate that the profession is regulated, not in a purely bureaucratic sense, but that valuers perform their task in an organised manner, not in a maverick or inspirational way, that they take care to educate themselves, and that they are subject to discipline.

(iii) Valuers need to be able to express more clearly what they do and what they do not do. It is not possible to 'make clients understand', nor is it tenable to urge that 'clients should be educated'. Care and precision in explanation will do much to achieve both ends.

(iv) Valuers need to improve the technical element of their skill, updating and extending their mathematical models, their access to and use of data, and their expression of the relativities of their judgement. They should not assume their task to be limited to the production, as if from a hat, of a final figure.

The main proposals of the Mallinson Report are that there be a greater dialogue between valuers and their clients leading to clearer instructions, a summary of which would accompany the valuation figure. A second proposal is the right for valuers to ensure that shareholders receive the statement explaining property valuations in company accounts. In addition, the report proposed closer liaison between valuers and auditors, with direct access to audit committees. In addition, the report proposes that there be increased investigatory powers for the RICS in cases of public concern or at the client's request. The report recommends that valuations need to contain more comment on valuation risk factors, price trends and economic factors. Refined discounted cash flow techniques and research on concepts of 'worth' need to be developed. Finally, the report also suggests that there be a wider availability of data, which is necessary for valuations, and that the definition of open market value should be retained but its title changed to 'defined value' or 'defined notional price'. The report embraced open market value (OMV) and estimated realisation price (ERP) and suggested a new possible basis of defined accounting value (DAV); however, this latter definition was rejected by the RICS group who prepared the new 'Red Book' although both concepts of OMV and ERP are embraced (Rich, 1994). It is hoped that these proposals would go some way towards dealing with the disquiet which has arisen over a number of cases. It is to be noted that this is not just a problem of valuation in the UK, as can be noted from the collapse of the Jurgen Schneider Property Group in Germany in 1994. This collapse is likely to have a lasting effect on the German property market because of the magnitude of the losses. Some of the blame relating to this collapse has been put on the poorly trained and organised German valuers whose valuation methods and education were suggested to be below those of the international standard. A German society of valuation surveyors has been formed to correct this.

The Mallinson Committee report advised that the previous 'Red Book' (guidelines used for valuing assets) and the 'White Book' (guidelines used for mortgage valuation and other specialist areas) should be merged. In September 1995 the Royal Institution of Chartered Surveyors' *Appraisal and Valuation Manual* was published (RICS, 1995). This manual provides the minimum required standards expected of professionals in practice and is mandatory from January 1996 onwards for members of the appropriate valuation institutions (the RICS and the Institute of Revenue Rating). The new 'Red Book' is in two parts: the Practice Statements and the Guidance Notes, The Practice Statements apply to all types of valuation and are mandatory, along with the appendices. The Guidance Notes are not mandatory but provide information on good practice. The 'Red Book' contains a number of definitions, previously discussed, including:

- *Appraisal*: The written provision of a valuation, combined with professional opinion or advice on the suitability of the subject property for a defined purpose.
- *Estimation of worth*: The provision of a written estimate of the net monetary worth of the subject property to the client.
- *Valuation*: The provision of a written opinion as to the price or value of the subject property on any given basis. It is specifically not a forecast, which in turn is defined as the prediction of the likely value on a stated basis at a future specified date. The complexity of the number of valuation definitions now being used is shown in Table 4.1.

These valuation bases are agreed with the client prior to the valuation and should be appropriate to the client's needs but cannot override statutory definitions. If ERP is required it is also necessary to provide market value or open market value. The calculation of worth is distinguished from calculations for market value or open market value. Open market value starts from the assumption that parties to the transaction acted knowledgeably, prudently and without compulsion. Market value appears to be the same as open market value but is given the definition used by the International Valuation Standing Committee (Estates Gazette, 1996). The 'Red Book' defined open market value as:

> An opinion of the best practice at which the sale of an interest in property would have been completed unconditionally for cash consideration on the date of valuation, assuming:
>
> (a) a willing seller;
> (b) that, prior to the date of valuation, there had been a reasonable period (having regard to the nature of the property and the state of the market for the proper marketing of the interest) for the agreement of the price and terms and for the completion of the sale;

Table 4.1 Valuation bases under the 'Red Book'

Base Definition	Application of Valuation Bases		
	Rental Value	Plant and Machinery	Other
Market value (MV) Open market value (OMV)	Open market rental value (OMRV) **(1)**. Valuer assumes the grant of a new lease, not a renewal	Open market value for plant and machinery (OMVPM)	
Existing use value (EUV), which is OMV subject to additional assumptions as to use		Valuation of plant and machinery to the business (VPMB) **(2)**	Existing use value for registered housing associations (EUVRHA)
Estimated realisation price (ERP) **(3)**	Estimated future rental value (EPRV) **(1)**	Estimated realisation price of plant and machinery (ERPPM)	
Estimated restricted realisation price (ERRP) **(4)**		Estimated restricted realisation price of plant and machinery (ERRPPM)	Estimated restricted realisation price for the existing use as an operational entity having regard to trading potential (ERRPEU)
Depreciated replacement cost (DRC)			

Notes:
(1) New valuation bases.
(2) Value of plant and machinery to the business is approximately the same as EUV.
(3) Estimated realisation price requires the valuer to consider what changes are likely to occur in the market for the property during the marketing period; this includes external factors such as quality of the location etc. It is the open market value but with completion assumed after the date of valuation and where the valuer is required to specify an appropriate marketing period.
(4) Estimated restricted realisation price is not forced sale value (which should not be used in any circumstances) but is where the estimate is subject to a marketing period defined by the client and which does not allow for proper marketing.

(c) *that the state of the market, level of values and other circum-stances were, on any earlier assumed date of exchange of con-tracts, the same as on the date of valuation;*

(d) *that no account is taken of any additional bid by a prospective purchaser with a special interest; and*

(e) *that both parties to the transaction had acted knowledgeably pru-dently and without compulsion.*

[RICS (1995), Practice Statement 4.2.1, p.4]

The 'Red Book' is divided into Practice Statements and Guidance Notes. Practice Statement 1 covers appraisal and valuations for all purposes includ-ing Home Buyers Reports and mortgage valuations. Practice Statement 2 relates to the requirement to understand the needs of the client and sets down the basic criteria that the valuer would need to identify. These cri-teria are the basis of valuation; the subject property; the purpose of the valuation; any assumptions to be made; and the date of the valuation. In addition, it should be clear firstly, whether information will be required from the client for the valuation to be made; secondly, the currency of the report; and, thirdly, the limitations to third party use and restrictions on publica-tion. Practice Notes 5–7 go on to examine special circumstances related to the report, the database of comparables, the record of analysis and, finally, the minimum requirements of the reports (for instance, the need to check whether the valuation report being provided will be included in the company accounts). Statements 8–22 list special requirements for reports if these conflict with general guidance given.

There is a continuing debate about estimated realisation price (ERP) and whether it will resolve or compound problems of credibility which gave rise to the need for the Mallinson Report in the first place. A view is that need for the valuer to look forward in providing valuation advice has been imposed on the profession by lending institutions and could result in more, rather than fewer, claims for negligence against valuers. The change for the profession relates to the way the old 'Red Book' referred to relevant ex-perience, while the concentration in the new 'Red Book' is on knowledge, understanding and skills (Estates Gazette, 1996). The new definition of ERP was needed following pressure from secured lenders who believed that the existing definition of open market value required the marketing period to be retrospective, ending at the date of valuation and expecting the valuer to look backwards. The valuer was therefore telling the lender only what, in effect, he already knew and did not supply what he wanted to know, which was an assessment of the security provided by the property in the future. The key differences are indicated in Figure 4.2 and Table 4.2. It is apparent in the market that some valuers are looking to forecast in situa-tions where they may not have the skills and knowledge to do so.

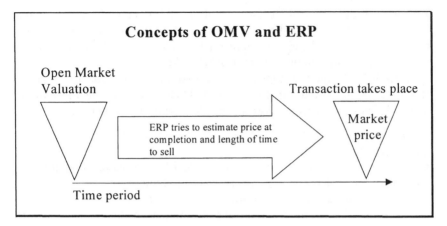

Figure 4.2   *Concepts of OMV and ERP*

Table 4.2   A comparison of open market value and revised ERP (source: Law and Gershinson, 1995)

Open market value	Revised ERP (from 1 January 1996)
Sale . . . completed . . . at the date of valuation **plus** proper marketing, agreement of price etc. prior to the date of valuation	*Opinion as to . . . consideration on the date of valuation . . . Completion of sale on a future date specified . . . following the period of marketing*
Both parties had acted knowledgeably, prudently and without compulsion (with effect from 1 January 1996)	Both parties **will** act knowledgeably, prudently and without compulsion

Law and Gershinson (1995) suggest that a valuation report should be an appraisal with emphasis on the risks attached to the performance of the property during the period of a loan granted as a result of the valuation. However one has to assume a static market unless the valuer or market as a whole is aware of factors which may affect the market, and if this is so then surely the market would have taken this into account. There may be concern that some valuers are forecasting valuation figures in the future, making assumptions regarding changes in the market that did not reflect the worth of the property at the date of valuation. The advice concerning the new ERP is to respond to the question of how much do you think the property can be sold for, commencing the selling process at the date of valuation, while indicating how long it will take.

In the light of the new regulations, the Appraisal and Valuations Board of the RICS suggested the following vital questions for the professional valuers to ask themselves before proceeding with an instruction:

- Do I know whether the mandatory requirements of the manual apply to the sorts of valuations I do?
- If I work regularly for the same client, do I have standard conditions of engagement which comply with Practice Statement 2?
- Have I prepared revised standard terms of business?
- Am I satisfied that I meet the qualification requirements in Practice Statement 5?
- Am I aware of the valuation bases to be adopted, and of the changes in some of the titles and the definitions? Have I put in hand amendments to my software?
- If my reports are to be referred to in published documents, am I ready to provide a draft statement for the purposes with my report, in accordance with Practice Statement 7.10?
- Do I know what service my client requires of me (see Practice Statement 2.1)?   [CSM, 1995b].

A recent joint study between the City University Business School and the Universities of Reading and Western Sydney was carried out on valuation reports, their format and the information provided. The study concluded that UK clients were generally satisfied with the quality of valuation reports received from external valuers but a common criticism was that valuers do not provide sufficient information on valuation methodology and the state of property and wider markets. The research noted that, in respect of the response from bankers, 77 per cent wanted more professional/industrial guidelines, this despite the introduction of Valuation Guidance Note 12 (VGN 12) in the new 'Red Book', already discussed, which gives detailed guidance to valuers on loan valuations (CSM, 1996).

4.4 SOURCES OF INFORMATION FOR THE VALUER ON THE WEB

There are a number of useful Websites for valuers; some of these are listed below. *Chartered Surveyor Monthly* provides details of some of these sites from which the information has been obtained (CSM, 2000):

EGi (*www.egi.co.uk*)   A subscription service of the *Estates Gazette*. Subscribers are given access to news stories from1995.

RICS (*www.rics.org.uk*)   The Website of the Royal Institution of Chartered Surveyors which gives detail of the profession and research.

Property mall (*www.propertymall.co.uk*)   A site with useful links to matters of property interest.

BCIS (*www.bcis.org.uk*)   The site of the Building Cost Information Service providing details of construction costs.

HM Land Registry (*www.landreg.gov.uk*)   Shows the work of the Registry and also has residential property price reports from 1995.

SUMMARY OF CHAPTER

This chapter has examined the role of the valuer and has looked at:

* The process of valuation.
* Types of valuation: statutory and non-statutory, open market value.
* The 'Red Book' of the RICS – the *Valuation and Appraisal Manual.*

REFERENCES AND BIBLIOGRAPHY

Baum, A. and Crosby, N. (1995) *Property Investment Appraisal*, Routledge, London.

Chartered Surveyor Monthly (CSM) (1995a) 'Finding your way into the new Red Book', *CSM*, October, p.22.

Chartered Surveyor Monthly (CSM) (1995b) 'Finding your way into the new Red Book' *CSM*, November/December, pp.20–2.

Chartered Surveyor Monthly (CSM) (1995c) 'Mallinson delivers a yorker', *CSM*, November/December, p.48.

Chartered Surveyor Monthly (CSM) (1996) 'The variable value of property investment valuation reports', *CSM*, April, pp.38–9.

Chartered Surveyor Monthly (CSM) (2000) 'Useful websites for surveyors', *CSM*, February, p.23.

Estates Gazette (1996) 'The new Red Book', *Estates Gazette*, 6 January, pp.96–7.

French, N. (1994) 'Editorial: Market Values & DCF', *Journal of Property Valuation and Investment*, Vol. 12, No. 1, pp.4–6.

Jenkins, S. (1996) 'Valuations still highly variable', *Estates Times*, 15 March, p.2.

Law, D. and Gershinson, J. (1995) 'Whatever happened to ERP?', *Estates Gazette*, 16 September, pp.164–5.

Rich, J. (1994) 'The wonderland of OMVs, ERPs and DAVs', *Estates Gazette*, 26 November, pp.153–5.

Royal Institution of Chartered Surveyors (RICS) (1992) *Statement of Asset Valuation Practice and Guidance Notes*, RICS, London.

Royal Institution of Chartered Surveyors (RICS) (1994) *President's Working Party on Commercial Property Valuations (Mallinson Report)*, March, RICS, London.
Royal Institution of Chartered Surveyors (RICS) (1995) *RICS Appraisal and Valuation Manual*, RICS, London.

Part 2:
Methods of Valuation

5 The Methods of Valuation

5.1 The five methods
5.2 The profits method
5.3 The contractor's method

AIMS AND OBJECTIVES

This chapter introduces the basic methods of property valuation: the five methods of valuation. The five methods are described and the profits and contractor's methods are dealt with in detail.

Key terms

Profits method – valuation based on the profits of an enterprise.
Contractor's method – valuation based on the cost of construction rather than value.

5.1 THE FIVE METHODS

The five traditional methods of valuation are the comparison method, the profits method, the contractor's method, the investment method and the residual method. The first three are dealt with further in this chapter, but the investment and residual methods are important enough for each to have a separate chapter of its own (see Chapters 6 and 7). The investment method forms the basis of the investment appraisal, a more general term for the whole range of valuation and analysis that a property professional might undertake. The residual valuation in the same way represents the core of the development appraisal. The methods can be distinguished as follows:

- The *comparison method* compares the capital values and rents of properties that have recently been sold or let with the subject property.
- The *profits method* is based on the assumption that the value of a property is based on the profit produced and is used in hotels for instance.

- The *contractor's method* is based on the cost of construction and is used where there is no market.
- The *investment method* is used to value capital investments in property; the approach to this form of valuation including the use of the Year's Purchase to capitalise rental figures has been examined earlier.
- The *residual method* is used in development situations and is based on value less cost and profit, and gives a balance to purchase the land.

The bases of the valuation methods

There are three bases to the valuation methods:

VALUE	COST	PROFIT
Based on: • Valuation of the property • Capital value or capitalised from a rental income *Use*: Comparison method Investment method Residual method	*Based on*: • Cost of contruction • Value on the basis of cost *Use*: Contractor's method	*Based on*: • Profit from accounts • Value on the basis of profits *Use*: Profits method

The use of valuations will differ according to whether they are being applied to existing property or new development, and the methods used in each case will differ too, as shown in the following:

For existing property	For new development
Use: Comparison method Investment method	*Use*: Comparison method Investment method Or use Value less Cost = Residual method

The comparison method

The comparison method will give rent and capital value; the investment and residual valuations will give capital value. Comparison is done by the analysis of transactions in the market; in the user market the aim will be to derive a market rental per m^2 and in the investment market a capital value could be derived. The art of the comparison method is the discovery of relevant data and the subsequent analysis. As property is unique, the problem lies in the adjustment to be made to the comparable to fit the property being valued.

5.2 THE PROFITS METHOD

The profits method is used where a premises' value is based on the profit produced by the business operating in the premises. The profits generated by the business will be contained in the company accounts, which will need to be analysed to produce the figures for the calculation. The accounts are an important means of assessing the performance of the business occupier and this performance would be crucial in the valuation. This approach underlines the importance of understanding company accounts which, besides being used in this method, are also important to the property professional in a number of different ways, for example:

- assessing the financial standing of a partner in a property development scheme;
- assessing the quality of a prospective tenant for letting purposes;
- assessing, for property management purposes, the standards of a contractor who would carry out works and provide services;
- assessing the security of a borrower in a property loan situation;
- assessing the standing of a company in which you propose to invest;
- assessing the standing of rival firms in the market with whom you, as a professional practice or company, may wish to take over, to be taken over by, or to merge with.

So, as one can see, there is a great need to understand the basic company accounts, and this analysis is covered in Chapter 15. The analysis of the accounts will show:

1. How well the business is performing relative to its costs (indicated by the **profit margin**).
2. How well it keeps its costs down (indicated by its **productivity**).
3. How well it competes with other firms (indicated by its **profitability**).
4. How well it is doing compared to other competing investments (indicated by the **return on capital**).

The calculation is shown in Example 5.1.

Example 5.1: The profits method

Gross earnings
Less cost of purchases **(direct costs)**
Gross profit
Less expenses   **(indirect/overhead costs)**
Net profit
Less return on capital for business
Annual rental value
Times multiplier
Capital value

Notes:
1. The net profit can be divided between the business and the property. The business part represents the **goodwill** of the business; the property part represents the **rental**.
2. The **goodwill** of a business is attached to the business, not the property, and represents the value of the existing trade and name of the company which is a product of public attitude and ongoing customer loyalty.
3. Note that goodwill is an **intangible asset** of the company as opposed to the building, plant and machinery, which are tangible assets. Other examples of intangible assets are patents or royalties.
4. The capital value of the business, as separate from the property, is assessed by adding the goodwill to business capital invested (stock, fittings and cash). This is the **going concern value** of the business.

The profits method is often used where there is an element of monopoly and the clear application of this method is shown where it is the operation that has the value itself, rather than the premises occupied. Some examples should clarify this; for instance, a fairground and racecourse are examples where the operation generates the income and land values otherwise could be low in their existing uses. Other examples are derived from good locations, which means that an operation could dominate that type of activity in the particular area concerned. A town may have only one cinema or bowling complex for instance. Certain locations may only have a single petrol filling station. Motorway locations offer monopolistic trading for filling stations, restaurants and other facilities, as do railway stations for newsagents. Monopoly may be a legal one or subject to a licence or franchise, hence one post office per village or one licence for a public bar or nightclub in a certain location. Statutory monopolies which generate income might also be valued in this way, but with public sector buildings we would probably be looking to a cost approach, discussed later, as there is unlikely to be a market for the property in the existing use.

The accounts need to be analysed and thus should be accurate, with appropriate auditing procedures having been carried out. The accounts need to be reviewed for the last 3–5 years to investigate any aberrations or extraordinary items. The analysis of the accounts should give a picture as to whether the business is being run efficiently, and comparisons can then be made on a local and regional basis for the activity; for instance, is the profit made per hotel room comparable to the industry benchmark in that locality? At the same time the opportunity cost of the activity should also be looked at, this being the cost of not getting a return, say, by investing in traditional investments. If you can obtain say 5 per cent in a building society, then why is a restaurant only earning 4 per cent? In this case, is the activity worth doing or is the situation one where the business is a start-up with low returns initially but the potential hopefully for greater earnings? The analysis of the accounts will provide key ratios for comparison and analysis. This is discussed in more detail in later chapters but essentially the analysis is shown in Box 5.1.

The return on the capital investment gives a clear indication of the performance of the company and in turn this is made up of two key ratios analysed from the accounts. This relationship is shown in Box 5.2.

BOX 5.1: THE KEY RATIOS

The key ratios used to analyse the profitability of an enterprise
 (i) Trading profit as a percentage of turnover.
 (ii) Profit before interest and tax as a percentage of average capital employed.
 (iii) Earnings per share, either basic (based on issued share capital) or fully diluted (based on authorised share capital, which is the total share capital that can be issued).
 (iv) Dividend per share.
 (v) Number of times covered – that is, the number of times a dividend is covered by earnings. This is also a measure used by property managers to assess the security of a tenant by calculating the number of times the rent is covered by the net profit of the tenant company.
 (vi) Assets per share – the asset backing of shares based on the value of the net assets divided by the number of shares. There has been much discussion in this area in relation to the share price of property investment companies, as one would expect the asset value per share to relate to the market price of the share. However, traditionally the market has discounted the net asset values of property investment companies historically by an average of approximately 20 per cent. The discount is measured by:

$$\frac{\text{Share price} - \text{Net asset value per share}}{\text{Net asset value per share}} \times 100\%$$

[Isaac and Woodroffe, 1995]

Example 5.2: A detailed calculation using the profits method

A1	B	C	D	E	F	G	H
2	This calculation has been done on a spreadsheet, the equations used in key						
3	cells (boxes) are shown in column H.						
4				£ pa			
5	Sales turnover			500,000			
6	Less purchases			300,000	Gross		
7	**Gross profit**			200,000	margin =	40%	**E7 = D5 − D6**
8	Less running costs				(sales/gross profit)		
9	Wages						
10	Repairs						
11	Insurance						
12	Rates (property taxes)						
13	Heating and lighting						
14	Insurance						
15	Vehicle expenses						
16	Stationery and postage						
17	Telephone charges						
18	Total			100,000	Net		
19	**Net profit**			100,000	margin =	20%	**E19 = E7 − E18**
20	Less owner's salary			20,000	(sales/net profit)		
21	Less return on capital invested			80,000			**E21 = E19 − E20**
22	Fixtures		80,000				
23	Stock		40,000				
24	Cash		5,000				
25	Total		125,000				**E25 = SUM(D22 : D24)**
26	Return @	8%	0.08 *		* cost of borrowing		
27	Return			10,000			**E27 = D25*D26**
28	**Adjusted net profit**			70,000			**E28 = E21 − E27**
29	Allocate	50% to property		50% to business			**E29 = 1 − C29**
30							
31	**Property:** annual rental value			35,000			**E31 = E28*C29**
32	× multiplier			10			
33	capital value of			350,000			**F33 = E31*E32**
	property						
34							
35	**Business** profit			35,000			
36	× multiplier			2			
37	**value of goodwill**				70,000		
38							
39	**Going concern value**						
40	Property				350,000		
41	Goodwill				70,000		
42	Fixtures				80,000		
43	Stock				40,000		
44	**Going concern value**				540,000		**E44 = SUM(F40 : F43)**

BOX 5.2: RETURN ON INVESTMENT

Return on investment
This is defined as:

$$\frac{\text{Profit}}{\text{Assets}} \times 100\%$$

Thus profit is looked at as a percentage of capital, and this is further influenced by two further ratios comprising the **profit margin** (profit as a percentage of sales) and the rate of asset **turnover** (sales dividend by assets).

$$\frac{\text{Profit}}{\text{Assets}} = \frac{\text{Profit}}{\text{Sales}} \times \frac{\text{Sales}}{\text{Assets}}$$

or: **Return on capital = Profit margin × Turnover**.

Notes on profits method

This method, as mentioned earlier, is essentially used for monopoly situations, the usual types of monopoly being by location, a racecourse for instance, or by a legal monopoly. In a legal monopoly, the business may only be able to operate with a licence or franchise.

Gross profit

The profits used in this calculation should be those that a tenant of reasonable competence could make from occupation of the property.

Expenses

The expenses should include overheads, and the usual charges and will include any depreciation allowance for fixtures, fittings and equipment. The usual expenses would include wages, heating, lighting, insurance, telephone charges and cleaning, advertising, printing, postage and stationery costs. The expenses will **not** include rent, as the calculation of the profits method is working the appropriate rental value out. This deduction must not be made and if it has, for any reason, then it must be added back. Also ground rents would not be deducted nor any loan costs.

Tenants share of rental

The interest on the business owner's own capital in business is based on fixtures and fittings, equipment, furnishings, stock and cash. The business owner will also include remuneration for the time and effort in running the business.

RICS Guidance Notes on the profits method

The RICS in Guidance Note 7 'Trade Related Valuations and Goodwill' gives the following guidance for the use of the profits method:

- the accounts need to be analysed, both current accounts and previous years' accounts, and projections need to be made for future years;
- the analysis needs to consider a maintainable level of trade and future profit;
- the analysis needs to identify potential purchasers.

Thus the valuation needs to be on the basis of recent current performance and future trading potential. The basis of valuation needs to be defined. The market, when using the profits method, needs to be analysed closely and, because of the specialist nature of the market, this analysis needs to look in detail at the behaviour of buyers and sellers in the market. The approach requires investigation of the most probable type or class of purchaser having regard to the nature of the business, its size and type of operation. The most appropriate calculation techniques need to be adopted in the light of these variables.

5.3   THE CONTRACTOR'S METHOD

The contractor's method or contractor's test is a cost-based approach to valuation used in rating and compulsory purchase; it is not generally used in the UK but is used in other countries in situations where there is no market. There are complex statutory arrangements in the People's Republic of China, for instance, in the implementation of their cost-based approach to the valuation of their real estate. In the application of this method, no account is taken of the development potential and the method is applied to property that rarely comes onto the market. Examples of where you would apply this approach include hospitals, schools, churches and power stations.

The valuation is based on the cost of building *less* obsolescence and depreciation *plus* the site value. The approach recognises the value of the site for the particular use, but as there is no market then it is the cost of the building that is taken into account. This produces a value for a new building; older building costs will require an adjustment to represent depreciation (the wearing out of the building fabric) and obsolescence (the inability of older building to facilitate optimum performance, as expected by current standards of design and technology and the present-day economics of location and use). The valuation is shown in Example 5.3.

Example 5.3: The contractor's method

Contractor's method
Building size $100,000\,\mathrm{m^2}$ @ £200/$\mathrm{m^2}$

replacement cost =	£20,000,000
Less Obsolescence @ 50%*	£10,000,000
Building value	£10,000,000
Plus Site value estimated at	£1,000,000
Value of property	£11,000,000

* Rate of depreciation/obsolescence is commonly in the range 10–60 per cent.

The method is used for certain types of building or uses where the properties rarely change hands in the market, or the properties may form part of a larger commercial transaction where the property element is only a small part. In these circumstances, analysis of prices in the market will provide little evidence for a useful valuation. Properties of this type are only offered on the open market where the building use has expired and the building or site can then be developed for a different use. The market is thus for an alternative use for the property, such as the conversion of a redundant church for residential use.

The examples in this category of valuation are usually public sector buildings or very specialist premises:

- *Quasi-public sector buildings* – such as churches, schools, libraries, fire, ambulance and police stations, army barracks.
- *Specialist buildings* – such as special manufacturing plants, airports (operational part, not shopping malls), oil-refining plants, sewage disposal plants, power stations.

The method is often considered as the method of last resort where other methods are inapplicable or impractical (Scarrett, 1991). The method estimates the replacement cost of the building together with the value of the land, and then adjusts the estimated replacement cost to reflect the age and inadequacy of the building. The use is important in rating valuation, compulsory purchase, as mentioned before, and, critically, in the valuation of company assets.

The use of this valuation in asset valuation is covered by a number of regulations. The Asset Valuation Standards Committee (AVSC) of the RICS has issued guidance notes related to asset valuation. This covers the issue of valuations in company accounts, Directors' Reports and other financial statements, and also when valuations are used for prospectuses and circulars relating to marketing investment. This approach is also used under the City Code for take-overs and mergers, and for insurance company purposes. The asset valuation was discussed in Chapter 4.

Fire insurance

The contractor's method is used to assess the reinstatement value of premises in case of destruction by fire and other perils. A fire insurance valuation is the full reinstatement cost and is determined on a basis of building cost prevailing at the time of reinstatement. To this value must be added other incidental costs such as architect's fees, loss of income to a landlord during the rebuilding period (if applicable) and the cost of alternative accommodation. Typically the property is measured and a cost per m^2 applied using a database such as the Building Cost Information Service (see Chapter 7 on the residual valuation). This service analyses current contracts for different uses and can thus offer a typical average cost that will need to be adjusted for location, quality and the scale of building. A further example of the contractor's method is shown in Example 5.4.

Example 5.4: The contractor's method

An operational premises has just been completed by a public sector body for its own use; it fulfilled the same purpose as an adjoining building which is 50 years old. Value the older building.

Value of new building:

Cost of land	£500,000
Plus Cost of building	£2,000,000
Value on cost basis	£2,500,000

Value of older building:

Cost of land		£500,000
Plus Cost of building	£2,000,000	
Less depreciation @	50%	
Depreciated cost		£1,000,000
Value on cost basis		£1,500,000

In Example 5.4, note that the value is markedly lower for the old property but that if we decapitalise the capital value to find an annual equivalent rental (to be used in rating perhaps), the rental values will be more similar. The reason for this is because we will decapitalise the capital value for the older property at a high yield to reflect the poorer condition, and this will reflect in decapitalising using a lower multiplier (see Chapter 6 on the investment method for more details of the capitalisation calculation).

For instance, for the *new* building:

Capital value   £2,500,000
Decapitalise @ 5%   divide by 20*
Annual equivalent rent   £125,000 p.a.

$$\left(\text{*Simply from calculation: } £2,500,000 \times 5\% = £2,500,000 \times \frac{5}{100}\right.$$

$$\left. = \frac{£2,500,000}{20}\right)$$

For *older* building:

Capital value   £1,500,000
Decapitalise @ 10%   divide by 10†
Annual equivalent rent   £150,000 p.a.

$$\left(^\dagger 10\% = \frac{10}{100}\right)$$

The 10 per cent is obtained by grossing up the net yield to reflect the depreciation of 50 per cent. So:

$$\text{Depreciated yield} = \frac{1}{(1-d)} \times \begin{array}{l}\text{normal yield, where } d \text{ is the rate of} \\ \text{depreciation (50\% or 0.5)}\end{array}$$

$$= \frac{1}{0.5} \times 5\% = 10\%$$

A much simpler way to understand is just to depreciate the multiplier by 50 per cent, thus 20×50 per cent = 10.

This shows some of the problems of cost-based calculations because, in practice, in the open market, the depreciated property would suffer from both a higher yield and a depreciated rent thus:

Rent of *new* premises   = £125,000
Rent of *older* premises = £125,000 × 50% = £62,500 p.a.

SUMMARY OF CHAPTER

This chapter has introduced the basic methods of valuation and, in particular, has provided an overview of the five methods of valuation. It has then concentrated on:

- The profits method.
- The contractor's method.

REFERENCES AND BIBLIOGRAPHY

Isaac, D. and Woodroffe, N. (1995) *Property Companies: Share Price and Net Asset Value*, Greenwich University Press, London.

Royal Institution of Chartered Surveyors (RICS) (1995) *Trade Related Valuations and Goodwill*, Guidance Note 7, RICS, London.

Scarrett, D. (1991) *Property Valuation: The Five Methods*, E. & F.N. Spon, London.

6 The Investment Method

6.1 The investment method of property valuation

6.2 The valuation of freehold interests

6.3 The tables used in the investment method

6.4 Exercises in the investment method

AIMS AND OBJECTIVES

This chapter explains the investment method of valuation and the use of tables in the calculation. It concludes by providing exercises in the method.

Key terms

Investment method – the capitalisation of net income using a multiple called the YP (Year's Purchase) to provide a capital value.
Net income – income less outgoings used in the investment method.
YP – a capitaliser based on the yield of the investment.

6.1 THE INVESTMENT METHOD OF PROPERTY VALUATION

To begin this chapter we must revise the investment method introduced in Chapter 1. Most investors seek to obtain a return on their invested money either as an annual income or a capital gain; the investment method of valuation is traditionally concerned with the former. Where the investor has a known sum of money to invest on which a particular return is required, the income can be readily calculated from:

$$\text{Income} = \text{Capital} \times \frac{i}{100} \quad \text{where} \quad i = \text{Rate of return required}$$

For example, if £1,000 is to be invested with a required rate of return of 8 per cent, the income will be:

$$\text{Income} = \pounds 1,000 \times \frac{8}{100} = \pounds 80 \text{ p.a.}$$

In this type of problem, the capital is known and the income is to be calculated. In the case of real property, the income (rent) is known, either from the actual rent passing under the lease or estimated from the letting of similar comparable properties and the capital value is usually calculated. The formula above has to be changed so that the capital becomes the subject:

$$\text{Capital} = \text{Income} \times \frac{100}{i}$$

What capital sum should be paid for an investment producing £800 per annum if a return of 8 per cent is required?

$$\text{Capital} = \pounds 800 \times \frac{100}{8} = \pounds 10,000$$

This process is known as 'capitalising' the income, in other words converting an annual income into a capital sum. It is essential that the income capitalised is 'net', that is clear of any expenses incurred by the investor under the lease, so therefore the formula can be modified to:

$$C = \text{NI} \times \frac{100}{i} \quad \text{where} \quad C = \text{Capital}$$

$$\text{NI} = \text{Net Income}$$

$$i = \text{Rate of return}$$

For given rates of return, $100/i$ will be constant, for example:

Rate of return	100/i
10%	10
8%	12.5
12%	8.33

This constant is known as the *Present Value of £1 per annum*, or more commonly in real property valuation, *Year's Purchase* (abbreviated to YP). The formula can thus be finally modified to:

$$C = \text{NI} \times \text{YP}$$

where C is the capital value, NI is the net income and YP is the Year's Purchase. The YP, calculated by using $100/i$, will only apply to incomes received in perpetuity, which are those received from freehold interests let at a full market rent or rack rent. Incomes to be received for shorter periods use a YP that must be calculated using a more complex formula, but tables of constants are available and *Parry's Valuation and Conversion Tables* (Davidson, 1989) are most commonly used. The traditional approach of Parry's Tables was to assume that the rental income was received annually in arrears, whereas in practice it is received quarterly in advance; although the tables have been modified, much traditional valuation uses the original assumption for simplicity. However, whatever income basis is used, the two essential elements required to perform the calculation are: the period of time that the investment is to last in terms of years, and the rate of return required, usually known as the all-risks yield (ARY).

To summarise, to estimate the capital value of an interest in real property using the traditional investment method, three elements are required:

(i) the net income to be received;
(ii) the period for which the net income will be received;
(iii) the required yield.

(i) and (ii) will be obtained from the lease of the subject property or, if the property is unlet, an estimate of the rental value will be obtained from lettings of comparable properties. (iii) will be obtained from analysis of sales of comparable investments. A valuer must therefore have knowledge of two separate markets: the letting and investment markets.

Example 6.1: An investment method calculation

Assume an industrial premises on the M25 London Orbital Road has a yield of 5 per cent. The net rental from the premises has been recently agreed at £100,000 p.a. How much would you pay for the freehold interest?

Net income	£100,000 p.a.
Year's Purchase @ 5% in perpetuity	× 20 YP*
Capital value	£2,000,000

$$^*YP = \frac{100}{Yield} = \frac{100}{5} = 20$$

In an investment valuation, some important factors should be noted. Firstly, even in owner-occupied property, a notional rent equivalent to a market rent is assumed to be passing, thus a rental value can still be assessed even if no rent is passing. Secondly, the full rental value is also termed a rack rental, which is the maximum rent for which a property can be let on the open market for a given set of letting terms; the more usual term is now either FRV (full rental value) or ERV (estimated rental value). Thirdly, the letting terms are an important consideration for the valuation; if a tenant is responsible for all repairs and insurance then the rent will be less than if the landlord is responsible. The usual situation is that tenants enter into lease where they have (in the terminology: 'they covenant to . . .') to pay for repairs and insurance. So the tenant covers all outgoings and this is called a fully repairing and insuring lease (a FRI lease). The landlord therefore does not have any outgoings and the rent is the net income. The rack rental on FRI terms is called the net rack rent.

The comparison method will give rent and capital value, while the investment and residual valuations will give capital value. The investment method thus converts the income from a property into a capital sum:

$$\text{Income} \times \text{Year's Purchase (YP)} = \text{Capital value}$$

$$\text{Income/Capital value} = \text{Yield}$$

$$\text{Yield} = 1/\text{YP}$$

Letting terms

Here is an example of a lease on full repairing and insuring (FRI) terms:

Rent	£10,000 p.a. (open market rental)
Repairs @ 15%	£1,500 p.a. (estimate of repair cost p.a.)
Insurance @ 2.5%	£250 p.a. (estimate)
Outgoings	£11,750 p.a.

Therefore the tenant's outgoings are £11,750 p.a. Other outgoings are property taxes (rates) and water rates, for which the tenant is usually responsible except in multiple letting situations where the landlord pays, apportions the cost between tenants and recovers the apportionment. Example 6.2 is of a lease on internal repairing terms (so the landlord is responsible for external repairs and insurance, and the tenant is responsible for internal repairs). The example shows the rent that the landlord would expect in these circumstances to put him in the same position as a FRI lease.

Example 6.2: Internal repairing lease

Expected rent on internal repairing terms:

Net income (net rent)	£10,000 p.a. (rack rent)
Repairs allowance	£1,500 p.a. (estimate of repair cost p.a.)
Insurance @ 2.5%	£250 p.a. (estimate)
Management fee	£1,175 p.a. (10% gross rent which includes repairs and insurance)
Expected rent	£12,925 p.a.

Rental terms

The open market rent is the rent at review and is also called the rack rent, full rental value (FRV) or estimated rental value (ERV). We will use full rental value from now on, but it is important for the reader to recognise the full range of terminology in use, and the other terms are also introduced depending on the source and purpose of the material. We need to distinguish between situations where the rent is historic and has been agreed some time ago. In an environment where there is economic growth and/or inflation, we may expect the rental to rise. Thus at the rent review, this historic rent will be reviewed to the full rental value (FRV). This known as a reversion. Traditional valuations do not explicitly calculate growth rate but base the valuation on the current open market rental, so the basis of the calculations is the FRV and in a reversionary situation would be called a reversionary rent; the rent before reversion is called the term rent. This is shown in Figure 6.1.

So, at stages during the lease, the rent could be reviewed. The normal lease is a 20- or 25-year lease with 5-year reviews, but reviews could be 3, 5, 7 or 25 yearly. The longer the review period, the higher the rent at review (because you have to wait a long time before you can review it again). To work out the rental value you need to compare the property you are working on with a comparable property using the comparison method. To compare properly you need to assess on a unit of comparison. The unit of comparison for most commercial properties is per square metre of space that is lettable space; for shops it could be per metre frontage and for land it could be per hectare. In the assessment of rental it is important to arrive

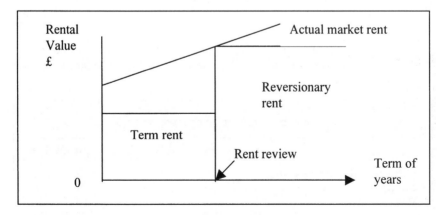

Figure 6.1 *Term and reversion rents*

at a net figure. In valuing an interest we are interested only in the net income (the income after outgoings have been paid) to the landlord. If rent contains amounts for outgoings, they should be deducted. So, rent *less* outgoings equals net income.

Outgoings

Outgoings are repairs, insurance premiums, general rates, water rates, general services and management costs, all of which need to be deducted from the gross rent to enable calculation of the net income used in investment valuation. In modern leases, the rent will already be net (FRI terms), as discussed earlier.

Repairs
Usually the landlord will get the tenant to do all the repairs. If the landlord is responsible, he may only have to deal with structural or external repairs. Repair costs should be costed but can be assessed as a percentage of rack rent as shown in Table 6.1.

Insurance
The property has to be insured for fire insurance which is based on the cost of the building (the reinstatement cost is based on the area of the building × the cost of construction per m^2). The premium is a percentage of the reinstatement cost but a rough approximation is 2.5 per cent of rack rent.

Rates
Rates are usually the liability of the tenant. The rates payable are the rateable value (RV) of the property times the rate in the £.

Management charges
These are made when there is a need to have a rent collector and to check that the tenant is in occupation under the terms of the lease (i.e. is abiding

Table 6.1   *Examples of repair costs*

	External %	Internal %
Offices and commercial	10	5
Shops	5	5
Residential	30	10

by the terms). If a net income is being received by the landlord (
FRI lease), sometimes a deduction for management is not made. Th
is 10 per cent of the rack rent but this may be reduced to 7.5 per
property that is easy to manage.

6.2 THE VALUATION OF FREEHOLD INTERESTS

The freehold interest is perpetual. The leasehold interest is for a number
of years during which the lessee or tenant has a right to occupy and enjoy
the property. This method used is the investment method as set out earlier
where:

- **Capital value** = **Net income per annum × Year's purchase**
- **Net income** = **Rent received per annum *less* Outgoings**
- **Year's Purchase** = $\dfrac{1}{\textbf{Yield}}$ (as a decimal)

Table 6.2 shows examples of historic ranges of yields; compare them with
the yields in 1996 shown in Figure 6.2. Although the yields do not appear
to vary widely, there is a range of values according to the type, location
and other factors of the property. This is an important lesson in obtaining
up-to-date information from the market: never rely on textbooks or out-of-

---

*Table 6.2   Examples of yield for different sectors (yields for freehold
interests let on a full rental basis) (Millington, 1984)*

Sector	Range of yields (%)	
Houses, poor	10	12
Houses, good	8	10
Flats	5	8
Factories/warehouses	6	14
Offices	4	9
Shops	4	9
Agricultural land	3	6
Ground rents with reviews	5	7

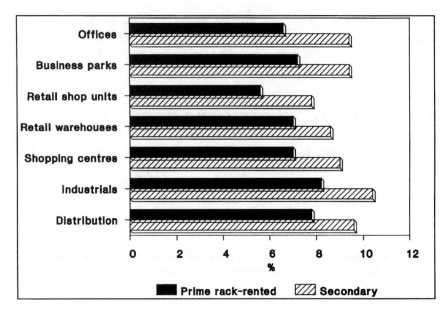

Figure 6.2 *Yields at April 1996*

Table 6.3   IPD initial yields (per cent)

Year/Sector	Retail	Office	Industrial
1995	7.1	8.3	9.5
1996	6.8	8.4	9.5
1997	6.3	7.7	8.7
1998	6.1	7.4	8.4
1999	5.8	7.0	7.8

date information but get up-to-date comparable evidence from the market to analyse.

The IPD (Investment Property Databank) UK annual index for 1999 (IPD, 2000) shows the initial yields given in Table 6.3 for the period 1995–99.

These yields are derived from the mean of the sample taken and thus the construction and scope of the sample are extremely important and are a critical part of the valuation exercise. As an example, the Valuation Office in the UK provides detailed data on transactions of which they are notified. Their *Property Market Report* provides these details. For instance, in the 6 month period to September 1998 it was notified of 159 transactions in shop properties in Britain: this sample was analysed to provide an average yield of 7.6, although the range was between 4 and 16.1 per cent (Valuation Office, 1998).

The basic valuation tables used in calculation are from Parry's Tables (Davidson, 1989) as explained earlier. The ones generally in valuations are summarised as:

(i) Year's Purchase single rate – used for the capitalisation of income into capital values.

(ii) Present value of £1 – used to estimate the present capital value of a future capital sum.

(iii) Year's purchase of a reversion in perpetuity – capitalisation of and income which is to be received in the future, commonly where a term and reversion situation exists (*see* earlier explanation).

The chosen method of valuation depends on whether the income is perpetual, variable or deferred. A perpetual income occurs where a freehold property is let at the full rental value. If we take a freehold shop let on full repairing and insuring terms at a rack rent of £5,000 p.a., the net income is £5,000 p.a., and this is already net because the tenant does all the repairs and pays the insurance. The income is received in perpetuity. The yield is assumed to be 7 per cent. The lease will not have rent reviews but we do not need to take into account rent growth if rent is at the full rental value as the yield allows for the growth:

Net income	£5,000 p.a.
YP in perpetuity @ 7%	14.286
Capital value	£74,430
	say £75,000

Zoning of shops

Zoning is a valuation procedure usually adopted in shops. The value reflects the different areas of activity in the shop, which thus earn more and are of more value. The front of the shop attracts customers into the shop and a lot of activity is carried on here, whereas to the rear of the shop the space may be used for storage and few customers may venture that far. This means that it may be a more effective valuation method to relate values to different areas, and to take a valuation for an area overall could be more correct.

Where shops are of equal depth in a shopping centre for instance, a valuation is based on a value per metre frontage of the shop. Usually however the zoning approach will be based on zones of 6 metre depth (although this may vary, traditionally it was on the basis of a 20 ft depth). Zone A is the front area of the shop and the values are halved back, usually to a zone B and then the remainder of the shop.

Corner shops with a return frontage may be valued at a higher-than-zone-A rent, depending on evidence. Large retail units with good circulation may not be considered appropriate for the zoning approach.

Example 6.3: Zoning

A shop has recently been let in a High Street for £5,000 p.a.; it has a frontage of 7 metres and a depth of 20 metres. You are asked to assess the rent on an adjoining unit that has a frontage of 8 metres and a depth of 18 metres.

Approach:

Valuation of comparable property:
Let zone A rental = x

Valuation			£
Zone A:	7m × 6m	= 42m² @ £x/m²	= 42x
Zone B:	7m × 6m	= 42m² @ £0.5x/m²	= 21x
Zone rest:	7m × 8m	= 56m² @ £0.25x/m²	= 14x
Total:	depth 20m		rent 77x

This rental = £77x = £5,000 p.a., therefore x = say £65/m²

Valuation of subject property:
Zone A rental = £70/m² from comparable

Valuation			£
Zone A:	8m × 6m	= 48m² @ £65/m²	= 3,120
Zone B:	8m × 6m	= 48m² @ £32/m²	= 1,536
Zone rest:	8m × 6m	= 48m² @ £16/m²	= 768
Total:	depth 18m		rent £5,424

This rental value of the subject property is **£5,424 p.a.** ✓

Examples of the investment method in use are shown in Examples 6.4 and 6.5.

Example 6.4: *An investment valuation*

Value the freehold interest in an office block of $50\,m^2$ at 1 High Street, which is vacant. 2 High Street is a block of offices of $100\,m^2$, just let at £10,000 p.a. on internal repairing terms. (The landlord is responsible for external repairs and insurance.)

Assumptions: office yield 7 per cent
lease to be on FRI terms

Approach:

Step 1: Capital value = Net income × YP; we know Yield, so we can calculate the YP (1/yield).

Step 2: We need to find the net income; the offices are not let, so this will be based on the rental of the adjoining property.

Step 3: Analyse comparable, and find rent per m^2 on FRI basis (net income).

Step 4: Do valuation.

Analysis of comparable 2 High Street:

	£	£
Rent received		10,000 p.a.
less:		
external repairs @ 10%	1,000 p.a.	
insurance @ 2.5%	250 p.a.	
management fee @ 5%	500 p.a.	
total outgoings		1,750 p.a.
net income		8,250 p.a.
net income per m^2	/100 m^2	
net income		82.5 per m^2

Valuation of 1 High Street:

	£
Net income:	
£82.5 × 50 m^2	4,125 p.a.
YP in perpetuity @ 7%	14.286
Capital value	58,929
	say £59,000

If 2 High Street had been sold at £137,500, then this would alter the valuation because the analysis would show that:

	£
Net income:	8,250 p.a.
YP in perpetuity	x
Capital value	137,500

$$YP\ (x) = \frac{137,500}{8,250} = 16.76$$

Yield = 1/YP = 6%

The valuation would then be redone at a 6 per cent yield.

Example 6.5: An investment valuation

An office block of $2,000\,\text{m}^2$ lettable area, let on fully repairing and insuring terms (FRI) and recently let at £200,000 p.a. has been sold for £2.8 million. You have been asked to value the freehold interest in a nearby office block that is to be let on internal repairing terms.

Approach:

Step 1: Analyse the comparable to work out the full rental value per m^2 and the yield.

Step 2: Value the subject property using the rent per m^2 and yield from the comparable. Adjust the rent for the different lease terms.

Analysis of comparable:

$$\text{Rent per m}^2 = \frac{£200,000}{20,000\,\text{m}^2} = £100 \text{ per m}^2$$

$$\text{Yield} = \frac{\text{Net income}}{\text{Capital value}} \times 100\% = \frac{£200,000\,\text{p.a.}}{£2,800,000} \times 100\% = \text{say } 7\%$$

Adjustments for subject property

Yield assumed to be 7.5 per cent (lease terms not so good as comparable because of repairing obligations).

Rent is $10,000\,\text{m}^2 \times £100$ per m^2 (from comparable) = £100,000 p.a. = net full rental value.

Gross rent will need to include repairs (£10,000 p.a.), insurance (£2,500 p.a.) and management (£5,000 p.a.); these costs are assumed.

Valuation:

	£	£
Gross income:		
(rent charged on an internal		
repairing lease)		117,500 p.a.
less: repairs	10,000	
insurance	2,500	
management	5,000	
Total outgoings		17,500 p.a.
Net income		100,000 p.a.
YP in perp. @ 7.5%		13.33
Capital value		£1,333,000

6.3 THE TABLES USED IN THE INVESTMENT METHOD

In Chapter 1 we looked at the constant known as the Present Value of £1 per annum, or more commonly in real property valuation, the Year's Purchase (abbreviated to YP). The formula was given as:

$$C = NI \times YP$$

where C is the capital value, NI is the net income and YP is the Year's Purchase. The YP was calculated by using $100/i$ and only applied to incomes received in perpetuity, which are those received from freehold interests let at a full market rent or rack rent. Incomes to be received for shorter periods use a YP that must be calculated using a more complex formula, but tables of constants are available and *Parry's Valuation and Conversion Tables* (Davidson, 1989) are most commonly used. In order to understand the basis of the traditional method and the calculation of compounding and discounting factors in investment calculations, we need to consider the tables that underpin the appraisals. In dealing with investment situations, we are considering the purchase of an asset to generate an income stream over a period of time. Thus we are converting the value of an income stream in the future into a present capital sum. The basis of the traditional approaches, the tables used in Parry's Tables, is about the conversion of present and future sums and the conversions of capital and income streams. The tables deal with the process of compounding and discounting; for instance, the Amount of £1 table will add compound interest to an initial sum to give a future capital sum. The six main options of conversion are:

- Capital to income and vice versa.
- Present sums to future sums and vice versa.
- The compounding of sums into the future, and discounting back to the present.

Summary of the valuation tables

Amount of £1

This table provides the amount £1 will accumulate to over n years at an interest rate of i per cent p.a. It thus compounds up from a present capital sum to a future capital sum. The approach is commonly known as compound interest and the formula is A (Amount of £1) $= (1 + i)^n$.

Present value (PV) of £1

The present value of £1 gives the sum which needs to be invested at the interest rate i to accumulate to £1 in n years. i discounts a future capital sum to a present capital sum; it is the process of the Amount of £1 in reverse and the formula is $1/A$.

Amount of £1 p.a.

This is the amount to which £1 invested annually will accumulate to in n years. It is thus compounding a present income stream to a future capital sum and the formula is $(A - 1)/i$.

Annual sinking fund (ASF) to produce £1

This is the amount which needs to be invested annually to accumulate to £1 in n years at an interest rate i per cent. It thus discounts back the future capital sum to a present income stream. The formula is $i/(A - 1)$.

Annuity £1 will purchase

This is the income stream that will be generated over n years by an original investment of £1. The income produced will be consumed as part capital and part interest on capital. Assuming the rates of consumption are the same, a single rate approach gives an equation $i/(1 - PV)$. If the rates differ, then the formula $(i + s)$ needs to be used, where s is the annual sinking fund formula above at a different interest rate from i. Note that this is the way a mortgage is calculated: the Building Society provides the initial capital sum and expects repayments of equal amounts throughout the loan period (assuming fixed rate money), but the repayments consist of interest and capital (that is, the sinking fund).

Present value (PV) of £1 p.a.

The present value of £1 p.a. is the present value of the right to receive £1 p.a. over n years. The future income stream is discounted back to the present value and is the opposite of the annuity calculation. Thus the formulation for a single rate is $(1 - PV)/i$ or for the dual rate, $1/(i + s)$, where s is the annual sinking fund at the sinking fund rate. This approach is commonly known as the Year's Purchase and gives the present value of a future stream of rental income.

Summary table

Option	Cash flow		Formula
	Now	**Future**	
Amount of £1 (A)	Capital sum	Capital sum	$A = (1+i)^n$
	compounding $\longrightarrow$		
PV of £1 (PV)	Capital sum	Capital sum	$PV = \dfrac{1}{A}$
	discounting $\longleftarrow$		
Amount of £1 p.a.	Income	Capital sum	$\dfrac{A-1}{i}$
	compounding $\longrightarrow$		
ASF to produce £1 (ASF)	Income	Capital sum	$ASF = \dfrac{i}{A-1}$
	discounting $\longleftarrow$		
Annuity £1 will purchase	Capital sum	Income	$\dfrac{i}{(1-PV)}$
	compounding $\longrightarrow$		
PV of £1 p.a. (YP)	Capital sum	Income	$YP = \dfrac{(1-PV)}{i}$
	discounting $\longleftarrow$		(single rate)

As a summary, we can see that the valuation tables may have a number of different uses in the analysis of investments, for instance:

Capitalising an income

As in the investment method of valuation:

Income × YP = Capital value
i.e. $i = 10\%$, $n = 10$ years, income = £10 p.a.
YP = 10 years @ 10% = 6.1446
£10 × 6.1446 = £61.46

YP compounds then discounts
i.e. PV of £1 p.a. =
Amt of £1 p.a. in 10 years @ 10%   £15.9374
× PV £1 in 10 years @ 10%   ×   0.3855
                                    ‾‾‾‾‾‾‾‾‾‾
                                    £6.1439

Discounting costs

Cost	£100
PV £1 in 10 years @ 10%	0.3855
Amount to be invested now	£38.55

Sinking funds

Estimating the contingency to be put away each year to pay for a future cost:

Future cost	£100
ASF 10 years @ 10%	0.0627
Annual sinking fund (ASF)	£6.27 p.a.

Mortgage instalments

The mortgage tables are based on the annuity that £1 will purchase. The annuity represents mortgage payments that are made up of instalments of interest and capital.

Discounted cash flow

These tables are used in investment analysis as already discussed:

- PV of £1 is used to discount capital sums.
- PV of £1 p.a. is used to discount incomes.

Annual equivalents

The tables can also be used for working out annual equivalents of capital sums, either capital costs or capital receipts (premiums).

A summary of the uses of the valuation tables is shown in Box 6.1.

6.4   EXERCISES IN THE INVESTMENT METHOD

Exercises in the use of the valuation tables and the investment method are set out below:

Valuation tables exercise

1. If £500 is invested at 9 per cent p.a., how much will have accumulated after 12 years?
2. How much would you pay today for the right to receive £7,000 in 6 years, using a discount rate of 11 per cent p.a.?
3. If £500 is invested each year at 9 per cent p.a., how much will have been accumulated after 12 years?

BOX 6.1: USES OF THE VALUATION TABLES – A SUMMARY

The tables used in the calculations have underlying formulae that have been given above. Any calculation can be carried out by a number of methods:

- Using the tables to look up the relevant multipliers.
- Using the equation which underpins the multiplier and using a calculator to do the arithmetic (a financial calculator is best, but essentially the calculator must have a facility to raise a number to a power as the basis compound interest calculation requires this: $A = (1 + i)^n$). The calculations will thus use a function denoted x^y.
- Using a computer spreadsheet, such as Excel, to input the equations and do the calculation. The spreadsheet has a number of functions that can be utilised to make the input easier.
- Using a computer program that will carry out these functions; this will have been programmed professionally.

---

4. If a freehold property has a rental value of £2,000 p.a. and the yield for this investment is 8 per cent, what is:
   (i) the Year's Purchase and,
   (ii) the capital value?

Answers

1 This is calculating the amount of £500 in the future.
The formula for the amount of £1 is $(1 + i)^n$ where $i = 0.09$ $n = 12$
Amount of £500 = £500 × $(1 + 0.09)^{12}$ = **£1,406**

2 This is calculating the present value.
The formula for the present value of £1 is $1/(1 + i)^n$ where $i = 0.11$ $n = 6$

Present value of £7,000 = £7,000 × $\dfrac{1}{(1+0.11)^6}$ = **£3,742**

3 This is calculating the amount of £1 p.a.
The formula for the amount of £1 p.a. is $((1 + i)^n - 1)/i$ where $i = 0.09$ $n = 12$

Amount of £500 p.a. = £500 × $\dfrac{(1+i)^n - 1}{i}$ = **£10,070**

4 (i) Year's Purchase for a freehold is $\dfrac{1}{i} = \dfrac{1}{0.08} = \mathbf{12.5}$

(ii) Capital value = Net income × Year's Purchase
$$= £2{,}000 \times 12.5 = \mathbf{£25{,}000}$$

Investment method exercise

1. The net income from an investment is £500 p.a. in perpetuity. Investors in this type of investment expect a 6 per cent return. How much will the investor pay for the right to receive this income?
2. An investor has paid £25,000 for the freehold interest in a shop. The rent is equivalent to a 9 per cent yield on the capital invested. Calculate the rent.
3. An investor paid £15,000 for a shop. The net rental is £1,000 p.a. What is the yield on the investment?
4. The net income is £37,000 p.a. in perpetuity. Investors require a 9 per cent return. How much will an investor pay for the right to receive this income?
5. Explain what a YP is.

Answers

1 The net income does not require deductions for outgoings like repairs, management and insurance.
The return is 6 per cent and the income is in perpetuity, therefore:
$$\text{YP} = \frac{1}{0.06} = \frac{100}{6} = 16.667 \text{ YP}$$
Valuation:

Net income	£500 p.a.
YP in perp. @ 6%	16.667 YP
Capital value	£8,334

2 Price paid is the capital value = £25,000
Shop is freehold so the rent is received in perpetuity. Yield is 9%.
9% of £25,000 = £2,250 p.a. = rent
Or in valuation format:

Net income	call	£x
YP in perp. @ 9%		11.1
Capital value		£25,000

(= 1/0.09)

Therefore net income x = $\dfrac{£25{,}000}{11.1}$ = £2,250 p.a.

Note rent is net of outgoings. Any liability to repair, manage, insure or pay out costs would need to be added to get to an appropriate gross income:

Net income		£2,250 p.a.
add repairs @	10%	£225 p.a.
insurance @	5%	£113 p.a.
management fees @	10%	£225 p.a.
Gross income required		£2,813 p.a.

3 Capital value £15,000
  Net rental income £1,000 p.a.

$$\text{Yield} = \frac{£1,000}{£15,000} \times 100\% = 6.67\%$$

Valuation:

Net income	£1,000
YP in perp. @ $x\%$	y
Capital value	£15,000

$$\text{YP } (y) = \frac{£15,000}{£1,000} = 15$$

$$\text{Yield} = \frac{1}{\text{YP}} = \frac{1}{15} = 0.0667 = 6.67\%$$

4 Net income is £37,000 in perpetuity so property is freehold.
  9 per cent return is the yield on the capital cost.
  Need to find the capital value.
  Valuation:

Net income	£37,000
YP in perp. @ 9%	11.1
Capital value	£410,700

This is the price an investor will pay for the income.

5 A YP is a capitalising factor which converts a future stream of income to a present capital sum.
  It is the present value of an income of £1 p.a. discounted on a year-to-year basis at the yield rate.
  (Strictly, it is the income per period discounted on a period-to-period basis, so the same approach can be used so long as the income per period ties in with the number of periods used.)

SUMMARY OF CHAPTER

- This chapter has developed the investment method of valuation.
- It has explained the use of valuation tables.
- It has given examples of, and exercises in, the investment method.

REFERENCES AND BIBLIOGRAPHY

Davidson, A. W. (1989) *Parry's Valuation and Investment Tables*, Estates Gazette, London.

Investment Property Databank (IPD) (2000) *IPD UK Annual Index*, IPD, March.

Millington, A. F. (1984) *An Introduction to Property Valuation*, Estates Gazette, London.

Valuation Office (1998) *Property Market Report*, VO, Autumn.

7 The Residual Method

7.1 Introduction
7.2 The residual valuation
7.3 The decision to redevelop or refurbish
7.4 Costs-in-use

AIMS AND OBJECTIVES

This chapter sets out the residual valuation and its various components. The chapter also considers the decision to redevelop or refurbish and summarises the cost-in-use calculation.

Key terms

Residual valuation – method used to derive the site value or developer's profit in a development appraisal.
Cost-in-use – cost calculation which includes on-going expenditure as well as the costs of installation.

7.1 INTRODUCTION

This chapter will outline the development method of valuation called the **residual method**. Before explaining the method, a number of initial points need to be made:

1. The residual valuation is a calculation that estimates the completed development value and deducts costs and profit to arrive at a residual land value.
2. Such a method is prone to error and can result in a wide range of answers depending on the assumptions made, the quality of inputs and the nature of the calculation carried out.
3. A more suitable approach would be the use of a direct comparison method but the problem with this relates to the fact that the end value of the development will determine the land value. In practice, developers will envisage different development proposals and thus the end values

will vary, making direct comparison of projects and thus land values difficult.

4. The residual valuation can be used in cases where existing buildings or sites are redeveloped. In these cases, any buildings or substructures may require demolition. The valuation method can also be used for the calculation involving the refurbishment of buildings.

5. The basic calculation involves the deduction of all costs (except the land cost but including a required profit) from the development value to obtain the residual land value. If the land value is known or estimated, then the inclusion of this in the costs, once deducted from the development value, will provide the profit arising on the project. This profit in this calculation is called the *developer's profit*.

6. More sophisticated analysis, taking into account changes in the revenues and costs over the development period, can produce more realistic answers.

7. There is, however, a major problem with the residual valuation – this is the time element. Normal transactions in property could take up to 6 months to complete but there may be very long time-horizons involved in development projects. This long time-frame is a result of the time taken to: assemble the land for the development site; obtain possession of existing premises and demolish them; obtain planning permission; construct the building; and let or sell the completed building. These stages are the critical steps on the path of the development project, all demanding particular knowledge of technical and managerial expertise. Other activities, such as obtaining finance for the development and marketing the completed building, all take time and resources but could run in parallel with the critical activities.

8. There is a major error in calculating the finance rates used in the calculation. These finance rates are based on short-term market rates and include the element of inflation/growth. However inflation and growth are not built into the elements of the calculation, but generally values are conservatively calculated at the commencement of the project, as are costs. Inflation and growth can be built into the calculation but may cause greater inaccuracy.

9. A second problem of the financial side relates to the nature of the finance rate used. This is a loan rate and thus assumes 100 per cent borrowing. This assumption is conservative and puts a high price on the finance costs, which is not realistic. Any project needs to be funded by both debt (borrowed money) and equity (buyer's own money or shareholders' money). Commonly, as seen in house purchase, 30 per cent of the money is provided by equity and 70 per cent by debt. The point of this is that the rate charged on equity may be less than that of the debt, and

thus the overall rate (known as the weighted cost of capital) is less than the market rate for the debt money (Isaac, 1996).

Property development is, as indicated earlier, the process by which buildings are erected for occupation or for sale/investment. Owners may build premises for their own occupation, for example major retailers may erect supermarkets, alternatively property developers may construct the same type of buildings for lease or sale. The process may be the same although some aspects of the financial appraisal may be different. A building offered for sale or investment is driven by a profit motive, a building for owner occupation may be related to the profitability of the enterprise within the building and thus profit motivation may be redirected or constrained. Property development is much like any other economic activity, satisfying wants with the application of scarce resources. In the case of property development, the wants are for space to work in, sell from, live in and enjoy recreational activities in. The process by which buildings are erected to provide space employs the key factors of production. This involves land for the site, capital for purchase of the land and materials, labour to erect a building and manage the process, and the entrepreneurial talent of the property developer to initiate the process and bring the pieces together.

A simplified approach to property development from inception to completion would involve a number of stages. In the first case there would have to be a need for the space, either a direct demand from a potential owner–occupier or indirect demand as assessed in market conditions (demand outstripping supply and driving the price of space upwards). If a developer intends to develop a site then there would need to be a situation where the sale price or completed value exceeds the costs of development involved for the process to be initiated. This surplus profit, arising from the profit in the development and also the size of the profit, will need to reflect the efforts and risk of the developer as entrepreneur. If market research carried out on a proposed development shows sufficient demand exists, then the developer's architect can produce sketch plans for the proposals, as these will need to be discussed with the planning authority. In the UK, as in most countries, development of land is subject to restriction under planning regulations and this is the first hurdle in the development process. Generally, an informed planning consultant will be invaluable at this stage, by knowing the type and scale of development that may be acceptable to the local authority, and the consultant may also be able to negotiate the most advantageous bargaining position. In parallel with these sketch plans, an initial development appraisal is drawn up. On the basis of the scale and type of development, a value can be assessed and rough costs calculated, which would indicate a level of profit and whether it is worth continuing further.

This calculation is called a *residual valuation*. The costs of construction are usually assessed by comparison. There are databases and source books that analyse recent building contracts in different locations for different types of buildings. A cost per square metre can thus be calculated and applied to the gross internal floor area of the building (measured between the internal faces of external walls).

Further informal discussion with the planning authority will lead to a formal application to the planning authority. This application may be for outline permission (a permission indicating the type and density of the development) and subsequently for detailed permission. Once the detail of the scheme is known, then a detailed appraisal can be carried out. The planning application would require detailed drawings and these would now be complemented by additional drawings from the architect. In a traditional approach, the drawings are costed in a bill of quantities by the quantity surveyor. In the early stages of the design process, the quantity surveyor will prepare a preliminary estimate, probably using one of the methods described by Seeley (1996) (these methods include unit, floor area, cube, approximate quantities, elemental comparative or interpolation). The valuer will provide updated values, and rents and funds will be raised to purchase the site (if not in ownership) and also for the costs of construction and ancillary costs.

With finance provided, a building contract can be entered into and the building erected. At the same time, the valuer or agent will be advising on a marketing strategy and seeking possible purchasers or occupiers so that once the building is completed there will be a minimal period when the property is empty and not providing a return. The return will be an income if the property is let and retained as an investment, or as a capital sum if the building is sold. If the building is built and occupied by the owner as developer, then a notional rent can be assumed to be passing.

Development and value

Key terms

Gross development value (GDV) – value of completed development.
Existing use value (EUV) or current use value – existing use value before development.

Development value exists where land or buildings can increase in value by the application of capital. It may be that this arises from a change of use of the land permitted by planning permission but the property development process usually implies the application of capital in the form of works to the land. The residual valuation, one of a number of techniques of property appraisal that assess the profitability of the proposals, calculates the increased capital value of the land because of the proposals. From this value, the calculation deducts the costs of works and the original value of the land and buildings. In an economic sense, costs should include a 'normal' profit that reflects the risk and commitment of the developer, however, depending on the price paid for the land, an 'abnormal' profit may arise because of the particular circumstances. The analysis can be summarised thus:

Basically: **value − cost = profit**

However, the residual valuation differentiates between the cost of construction and the cost of the existing land/building – the existing use value (EUV). The value of the completed development is termed the gross development value (GDV).

Thus: **GDV − (building costs + EUV) = profit**

If the land value is known because it has been agreed as a purchase price, then this equation provides the calculation of the profit. However the general case is that the land cost is not known and thus the equation is rearranged:

GDV − (building costs + profit) = EUV

The EUV, being the existing value of land and buildings on the site, will thus determine whether or not a normal profit is earned. For instance, if the actual land cost negotiated is lower than the EUV determined by the above calculation, then the profit increases, assuming the other costs to be static, and an abnormal profit is achieved. The need to use a residual valuation approach arises because of the uniqueness of land and property as an asset class. This is reinforced by the uniqueness, in most situations, of development proposals for each site. If equal-sized plots were being sold in the same location with the same density and type of development, then a form of comparative analysis could be applied, a price per hectare for instance. In these cases, adjustments would need to be made in the comparison and these adjustments, depending on their scale and complexity, could easily undermine the use of comparable valuation. The residual method has been criticised by the Lands Tribunal (the highest court for dealing with property valuation and compensation issues in the UK) because of the number of variables in the calculation, and the assumptions and variances underlying the calculations used as inputs to the valuation. The residual valuation has to be used in practice in most cases, as we have said, because the components of the development value and the profitability of each project will differ dramatically depending on the type and scale of the development proposals. The main variables in the calculation are:

Value of the site:
   Depends on location, use (under planning law), topography, legal constraints, ground conditions, services and access (for example).

Value of the proposed development:
   Depends on demand, use, density, design, layout and infrastructure.

Cost of construction:
   Depends on size, shape and height, design, type of buildings, planning constraints on buildings and landscaping, site conditions, provision of services and access.

The extent of the variations in these factors means that each site may be unique and thus the calculation for the site value is a residual based on what can be achieved as development on the site. To summarise, there are two approaches to valuing the development potential of a site:

(i) *A comparative approach*
   This is useful if there are direct comparables of sales but this is unlikely in a complex development situation where each development and thus the potential of each site will be unique.

(ii) *A residual valuation*
   Here the gross development value is assessed either by a capital comparison approach or by the investment method (the capitalisation of an estimated future income flow using an appropriate multiplier). The net value from the site is calculated by deduction of the costs of building and a profit figure from the gross development value; this is thus a residual calculation.

As considered earlier, the traditional methods used in valuation are traditionally called the five methods:

- the investment method;
- the comparison method;
- the contractor's method (a cost-based method);
- the profits method; and
- the residual valuation.

The residual valuation, as we have already seen, is used in development situations but, in fact, this valuation may rely heavily on the other methods. It may use the investment method to determine the gross development value of the proposed development. It may use the comparison method to compare capital values or site values calculated with examples from the market. The costs calculated for building works are a form of the contractor's method approach. Depending on the type of property, the profits method may also be used to determine the gross development value.

Summary

A final point to be made, as discussed earlier, about the valuation of the site is that the value of land is determined by its use and intensity of use. Land may have development potential but it will require planning permission for any form of development except for some minor works and some changes of use. The Town and Country Planning Acts determine this process of granting permission to develop. The Town and Country Planning Act 1990 basically defines development as:

> *the carrying out of building and other operations on, under or over land.*

A residual valuation is very sensitive to slight variations in its different elements such as rent, initial yields, construction costs, finance rate and building period. Because of this, the Lands Tribunal has regarded this method as one of the last resort (First Garden City Ltd *v.* Letchworth Garden City Group, 1966).

7.2   THE RESIDUAL VALUATION

Simplified residual calculation

> The basis of calculation is:
> value of completed development
> *less* cost of carrying out development
> *equals* amount available to pay for the land.

This basis of calculation is shown in Example 7.1.

Example 7.1: A simplified residual valuation

Proposed office development: city centre site
Project details

Gross area	10,000 m²	Net lettable area, say 80%
Rental value	£200/m²	
Building cost	£700/m²	
Profit as a percentage of cost	20%	

Appraisal	£	£
1. *Gross development value:*		
Net lettable area	8,000	
Rental value/m²	200	
Rental income	1,600,000	
Yield (%) 10	10 YP	
Capital Value		16,000,000
2. *Development costs:*		
Building costs:		
10,000 m² @ £700/m²	7,000,000	
Fees, say	1,000,000	
Interest on costs, say	3,000,000	
Total cost	11,000,000	
Profit @ 20% cost	2,200,000	
Total cost plus profit		13,200,000
3. Amount left for land purchase		£2,800,000

This calculation has been redone to show the formulae which need to be used on a spreadsheet:

Spreadsheet example

	A	B	C	D	E	F	G	
1	Proposed office development: city centre site							
2								
3	Project details							
4	Gross area		10,000 m²		Net lettable, area say		80%	
5	Rental value		200/m²					
6	Profit as a % of cost		20.00%					
7								
8	Appraisal				£		**FORMULA USED**	
9		Gross development value:						
10		Net lettable area			8,000		**C4*G4**	
11		Rental value/m²			200		**C5**	
12		Rental income			1,600,000		**E10*E11**	
13		Yield @	10%		10	YP	**1/C13**	
14					16,000,000		**E12*E13**	
15		Development costs						
16		Building costs						
17		10,000 m²	@	£700.00	7,000,000		**B17*D17**	
18		Fees, say			1,000,000			
19		Interest on costs, say			3,000,000			
20		Total cost			11,000,000		**SUM(E17:E19)**	
21		Profit @	20%		2,200,000		**E20*C21**	
22		Total cost plus profit			.	13,200,000	**E20+E211**	
23		Amount left for land purchase				2,800,000	**F14–F22**	

Notes:
Cells C13, G4, C21 are formatted as decimals and will calculate as a decimal not a percentage so in G13 the formula is 1/C13 not 100/C13.

The costs in a residual valuation, which have to be deducted from the gross development value include:

- building costs and fees;
- fees on letting and advertising;
- interest on costs;
- contingencies;
- purchase costs of land (not the land value, as this is the residual). Purchase costs would include fees on purchase and compensation for tenants to obtain vacant possession.

These elements are discussed in more detail in the following sections, showing examples of costs and other elements of the valuation:

Table 7.1   Building costs (BCIS, 1999a)

	£/m²
Offices, general	792
Offices, with air conditioning	904
Offices, 6+ storey	1049
Shops, general	488
Shopping centres	508
Hypermarkets, supermarkets up to 1,000 m²	408
1,000–7,000 m²	660
Warehouse	354
Retail warehouses	332
Factories, general	370

1. Building costs

Building cost figures are averaged out from recent contracts involving work of the same type. The figures can be obtained from the Building Cost Information Service (BCIS). These are mean UK figures from the *Quarterly Review of Building Prices* (BCIS, 1999a) and are shown in Table 7.1. BCIS *online* provides continuous updated cost data in the UK to subscribers.

Costs per square metre are the national average tender prices for construction works (exclusive of external works, contingencies, professional fees and VAT) divided by the gross internal floor area of the project. The regional variation of costs for London was around +18 per cent in March 1999. VAT (Value Added Tax) is payable on new contracts, except housing, and on refurbishment contracts at 17.5 per cent but can be recovered where developers/builders are registered for VAT.

Gross internal areas are the gross areas measured from the inside of external walls – see the definition in Box 7.1. This measurement contrasts with other measures used in the development process. Planning matters are dealt with on gross external areas while rentals are sometimes dealt with on a net internal basis where common parts and services and access-ways are excluded. Rule-of-thumb guidelines for converting gross to net may be 0 per cent for new industrial/warehouses, 10 per cent for industrial property generally, and 20 per cent for shops and offices and older industrial units.

2. Fees

The fees are assessed at 12.5 per cent of costs to include architects', structural engineers' and quantity surveyors' fees.

BOX 7.1: DEFINITION OF GROSS INTERNAL FLOOR AREA FOR COSTING PURPOSES (BCIS, 1999a)

The gross internal floor area is defined as the total of all enclosed spaces fulfilling the functional requirement of the building measured to the internal structural face of the enclosing walls. It includes areas occupied by partitions, columns, chimney breasts, internal structural walls and the like. Also included are lift plant, tank rooms and the like above the main roof space. Sloping surfaces such as staircases, galleries, tiered terraces and the like are measured flat plan.

---

3. Contingency

This may be between 0 and 3 per cent, depending on the nature of the project, the contract for construction and possible risk of variation of cost. It is based on the total cost of building, including external works, fees and interest charges.

4. Finance charges

An allowance for finance charges is used; it is based on calculating interest on the total building cost for half the building period. This approximation represents the fact that not all the money for the contract will be required at the beginning of the contract but that money will be drawn down as work proceeds. The total cumulative cost is represented by the S-curve of construction costs over the building period (see Figure 7.1). For the fees, as these are front-ended in respect of the work done for drawings and cost estimates, the interest on fees is estimated as being over two-thirds of the building period.

The builder is paid monthly but the bank may assess interest on outstanding amounts on a monthly or quarterly basis, thus interest should be compounded on the same basis. On a simple analysis, simple interest is used and only compounded if the building period exceeds one year and then on an annual basis. The interest rate can be assessed as a margin over the base rate. One may use a margin of, say, 3 per cent to reflect the nature of the developer and scheme, giving, say, 9 per cent if the base rate is 6 per cent.

5. Letting fees

Generally these are 10 per cent of the initial rents to be received but if there are joint agents as on a larger scheme, they will operate jointly for a total fee of 15 per cent of the rents. Advertising, depending on the project, is, say, a spot figure of 0.5–1.0 per cent of the gross development value.

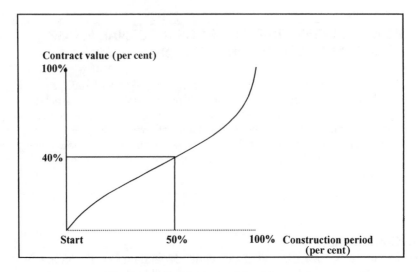

Figure 7.1 *S-curve of building costs*

6. Development period

The development period includes the planning period, the building contract and the void period. The planning period is the time required to get planning permission, drawings and building costs, assume, say, 6 months as an example. The void period is the time to let the property, which depends on circumstances. In this example, 3 months has been allowed, which is likely to be optimistic. This example assumes 9 months for the building contract. The application of finance to the phases of development is shown in Figure 7.2. From the figure it can be seen that interest is charged on the whole cost for the void period.

7. Gross development value

This is an investment valuation based on:

Net income from completed development × Year's Purchase @ development yield = Gross development value

8. Developer's profit

This is a percentage based on the Gross development value or total cost; Say, 20 per cent total cost or approximately 17 per cent Gross development value. These two figures are interrelated:

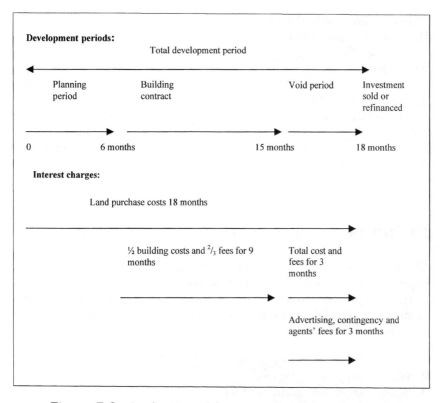

Figure 7.2 *Application of finance to development periods*

Gross development value (GDV) – Total cost (TC) = Profit (P)   (equation 1)

If $P = 0.2$ TC, then, rearranging, $TC = \dfrac{P}{0.2}$ (equation 2)

Inserting the value of TC from equation 2 into equation 1, equation 1 becomes:

$$GDV - \frac{P}{0.2} = P, \text{ thus GDV} = P + \frac{P}{0.2} = \frac{0.2P + P}{0.2} = \frac{1.2P}{0.2} = 6P$$

thus $P = \dfrac{GDV}{6} = 16.67\%$ GDV

9. Notes on residual valuation

There are so many variables in the residual valuation that inaccuracy can easily occur. Changes in the elements, especially the Gross development value, can dramatically alter the residual land value. Valuers can therefore alter the variables to determine the outcome as a form of sensitivity analysis; this is discussed later.

The residual calculation can be extended to devise a ground rent calculation in situations where there are partnerships between developers and landowners, and the developer takes a lease of the site. Ground rent is the common term for a rental arising to the owner of land when a lessee has the right to build upon the site.

7.3 THE DECISION TO REDEVELOP OR REFURBISH

The decision to redevelop or refurbish is thus a difficult one. Assume one requires a continuity of use then temporary accommodation may be required if premises require refurbishment or the development of new premises need to take place in parallel. The key questions that need to be asked are:

1. What is the total cost of construction?
2. What is the cost of the land?
3. What costs of relocation are there?
4. What values can be realised on sale?

If a building is being refurbished, then the site may already be owned but due allowance should be made for the value that the building would achieve if it were to be sold. An approach to this problem is shown in the next section.

The decision to redevelop/refurbish

Assume an office building requires refurbishment. To compare the cost with a redevelopment option one needs to consider the following costs:

Refurbishment
- Historic cost of premises
- *plus* Cost of refurbishment
- *plus* Disturbance costs

This can be compared to the development option:

Table 7.2 Example of the refurbishment decision against redevelopment

Refurbishment		New building	
Historic cost	0.1m	Cost	1.7m
Unrefurbished value	1m	Worth	2m
Cost of refurbishment	0.3m		
Refurbished value	2m		

Book profit if retained:
2m − (1m + 0.3m + 0.1m) = 0.6m

Realised profit if disposed of:
2m − (0.3m + 0.1m) = 1.6m

Book profit on completion:
2m − (1.7m) = 0.3m
plus 1m sale = 1.3m

Development
- Cost of site
- *plus* Cost of construction
- *plus* Cost of relocation
- *less* Sale of existing building

The two summaries in Table 7.2 give an example of the process. The total costs involved are shown but now need to be compared with the value of the premises on the completion of the work (that is, net value of the refurbished property compared to the net value of the new development). Value can be realised on disposal because property assets may appreciate. In this situation it is important to be careful how assets are accounted for, as assets are valued at market value.

7.4 COSTS-IN-USE

In the post-construction phase of a development, the valuation tables can be used for calculations of costs which can then be inserted into investment appraisals. The cost can be used to calculate an appropriate adjusted value. Costs and expenses, like income, are time-related and thus the approaches used to discount are the same. In this case, values are replaced by costs and are negative rather than positive cash flows. In reality, a net cash flow would be used in calculation for each time period. Example 7.2 shows a cost-in-use calculation.

Example 7.2: A cost-in-use calculation

Data

A client has purchased an industrial building for owner occupation at a price of £200,000. A building survey has been carried out and its present condition noted. A schedule of maintenance and repairs has been drawn up with the following estimates of cost:

- The annual repair and maintenance allowance is calculated at £20,000 p.a.
- The roof will require a major overhaul after 5 years at a cost of £30,000.
- The electrical system will require replacement after 2 years at a cost of £5,000.

Using current cost estimates and a discount rate of 8 per cent, estimate the total true cost of purchase.

Approach

- All costs need to be in terms of a present capital value.
- The purchase cost is a present value so no adjustment is necessary.
- The repair cost is a future annual cost to be adjusted to a present capital cost (this is the Present Value of £1 p.a. or Year's Purchase).
- The roof and electrical work are future capital costs which need to be discounted to present capital costs (Present Value of £1).
- The true cost is the total of the adjusted cost.

Calculation

The calculations use *Parry's Valuation Tables* or the equations shown in section 6.3.

True cost of purchase:				
1. Present costs				
Cost of purchase			£200,000	
2. Future annual costs				
Repair and maintenance		£20,000		
YP in perp.		12.5		
			£250,000	
3. Future capital costs				
Roof cost		£30,000		
PV £1 in 2yrs @ 8%		0.681		
Present capital cost			£20,430	
Electrical cost		£5,000		
PV £1 in 5yrs @ 8%		0.857		
Present capital cost			£4,285	
Total true cost of purchase			£474,715	

The calculation is simplified in the sense that in reality the repair cost would not go on indefinitely without refurbishment or demolition, and also the client may well move and sell on the property after a period of time. The calculation does give an approach to the whole cost associated with use of a building.

Exercise question

Discuss the use and limitations of the residual valuation.

Outline answer

The residual valuation is a method of calculating a residual site value in a development calculation by deducting the costs of development (including profit but excluding land costs) from the Gross development value (GDV). An example of the method is shown earlier in this section.

There are a number of problems with regard to this approach, which need to be discussed. There are so many variables in the calculation that errors easily occur. The answer is a residual and small variances in the major inputs to the calculation can magnify the changes in the residual. The inputs to the calculation are spot figures whereas ranges of figures with probabilities may be more appropriate. Finally, the calculation does not cope well with changes over time, in terms of rent levels, interest rates or the inflation of building costs, for example. This approach contrasts with a cash flow approach, which can reflect a stream of income or costs through the project. The cash flows can be divided into periods and a net inflow of cash or outflow, as the case may be, can be calculated.

SUMMARY OF CHAPTER

- This chapter has outlined a valuation approach to assist in development valuations by introducing the basic residual calculation and its components.
- Development valuations use a residual form of valuation that can be used to calculate the land value for the development site.
- An alternative, surer approach is to use a comparison approach to determine the site value. This may be impractical because the development value that determines the site value may be very different depending on the type of development envisaged.
- The chapter has also examined the economic decision to redevelop or refurbish and considered costs-in-use.

REFERENCES AND BIBLIOGRAPHY

BCIS (1999a) *Quarterly Review of Building Prices*, BCIS, issue no. 73, March.

BCIS (1999b) *Review of the Construction Economy*, BCIS, Web page (http://bcis.co.uk/review.html), 24 March.

Darlow, C. (ed.). (1988) *Valuation and Development Appraisal*, Estates Gazette, London.

Davidson, A. W. (1990) *Parry's Valuation and Investment Tables*, Estate Gazette. London.

Isaac, D. (1994) *Property Finance*, Macmillan (now Palgrave), London.

Isaac, D. (1996) *Property Development: Appraisal and Finance*, Palgrave, Basingstoke, Hants/New York.

Isaac, D. and Steley, T. (2000) *Property Valuation Techniques*, Macmillan (now Palgrave), London.

Marshall, P. and Kennedy, C. (1992) 'Development valuation techniques', *Journal of Property Valuation and Investment*, Vol. 11, No. 1, pp. 57–66.

Seeley, I. H. (1996) *Building Economics*, Macmillan (now Palgrave), London.

Part 3:
The Investment
Method

8 Discounted Cash Flow Approaches

8.1 A critique of the traditional methods of valuation

8.2 Capital appraisal techniques

8.3 Discounted cash flow approaches

AIMS AND OBJECTIVES

This chapter introduces a discussion of the traditional approaches to property valuation. It considers various approaches to capital appraisal. It then goes on to examine discounted cash flow approaches in detail.

Key terms

Discounted cash flow (DCF) – the discounting of future cash flows back to a present value.
Net present value (NPV) – the net present value of the discounted future cash flows.
Internal rate of return (IRR) – the discount rate which would give an NPV = 0.

8.1 A CRITIQUE OF THE TRADITIONAL METHODS OF VALUATION

The distinction between valuation and analysis

The property crash in the early 1970s focused attention on valuation methods used in the profession. Over the period since then, there have been a number of pressures on valuation professionals to improve the quality and standard of the valuations produced. This has arisen for a number of reasons. Large-scale investment, for instance, has taken place in recent years and the investment advisers acting for the institutions and investors are looking for more analysis in the valuations that have been carried out. Because of situations that have occurred in the past involving institutional investors, where actual returns on property investments have not reflected target returns set out to accord with the price paid, there has been much debate about the validity of the methods used. There is also much more awareness in the market now in terms of the responsibilities of the professional to clients' demands. Clients are now demanding that the property professional should not just act as an agent but provide, during the buying and selling process, some idea to the client of the forecast of income arising from the investment in the future.

This added awareness and monitoring of valuation procedures has been a subject of debate in the professional institutions as well as in the market-place. Recent suggestions by leading members of the RICS are that valuations should try to reflect a view of the future movement of prices, and to forecast potential supply-and-demand situations that may affect price levels. The findings of the Mallinson Report (RICS, 1994) on commercial property valuation suggested that the valuer should get clearer instructions from the client and should more clearly explain the valuation of property in company accounts. In addition, the report suggested that there should be more comment on valuation risk factors, price trends and economic factors, and the use of more refined discounted cash flow techniques. The recent debate and the earlier debates have combined to demand that, in what has previously been called property valuation, a more extensive service of property analysis be provided. Generally the approach that should be taken (see Baum and Crosby, 1995) is that the overall property appraisal should be clearly divided between property valuation for purchase, that is the valuation for market price, and the subsequent analysis of performance. In the first case, this is defined as valuation and in the second case it is analysis, the overall process being generally termed 'property appraisal'. Thus the valuation of a property, that is the calculation of the exchange value of property, is different from the subsequent analysis of the perfor-mance of the investment, which is the appraisal of its actual worth. Calcu-lations before and after purchase will not agree because of the lack of perfect knowledge in the market at the time of the transaction, and the inability to predict future changes in the cash flow and the risk profile of the investment accurately. Thus the techniques discussed later on in this book can be used to anticipate the market value, or else to record and analyse the progress of the investment subsequent to purchase. However, it is still important to understand the difference between these two approaches.

The argument of using discounted cash flow (DCF) approaches against the traditional 'Year's Purchase' investment method is extensive. Problems arise because the price paid in the market may not reflect the present worth of the future cash flows, and these problems relate to the fact that property appraisal needs to distinguish between the valuation for purchase price and the analysis of the worth of an investment. A DCF approach appears to be the only realistic approach to dealing with over-rented property where existing contractual rents under a lease that have been agreed in the past are now higher than those generally evident in the market for equivalent properties. In the present U.K. market, the use of traditional techniques may no longer be defended. The traditional methods may not be able to cope with issues such as rent-free periods, reverse premiums, tenant incentives, bad debts, negative growth and over-rented properties. So the use of the DCF should be paramount, although it needs to be applied appropriately; the DCF approach may be no more consistent than the conventional method, and both approaches require some modification to be used in a way that is compatible with basic economic concepts (French and Ward, 1995).

The application of valuation methodology requires the definitions to be clear and, on the basis of these definitions, the debate between the various methodologies can be clarified. The distinction between market price, valuation and worth must be clarified in this context and to a certain extent we have discussed this in Chapter 4. Baum *et al.* (1996) suggest the following approach:

- *Market price* is the recorded consideration paid for a property.
- *Valuation* is the estimate of the most likely selling price, the assessment of which is the most common objective of the valuer. This 'most likely selling price' is commonly termed 'open market value' in the UK but is different from the concept of worth.
- *Worth* is the underlying investment value and consists of two aspects. Firstly, *individual worth* is the maximum bid price of an individual purchaser. Such a bid would take into account the appropriate use of all available data relating to the individual, the property and the market. Secondly, *market worth* is the price at which an investment would trade on a market where buyers and sellers were using all available information in an efficient manner.

The application of these different concepts leads to adoption of different valuation approaches, Peto *et al.* (1996) have suggested that, in terms of market value, the valuer should adopt a model that gives most help in adjusting evidence for the inherent differences between one property and another, and gives the client the level of detail required. In this consideration they adopt a strategy covering the all-risks yield, the short-cut DCF and the full DCF:

- *All-risks yield*: In most cases, they argue, the all-risk yield approach concentrating on the initial yield is still the most acceptable approach. It is based on comparable evidence and thus, in markets where there is sufficient evidence, it can give the best indication of market sentiment.

- *Short-cut DCF*: For more complicated situations, or as a check on the all-risks yield approach, a short-cut DCF approach may be appropriate. This makes more rational use of comparable evidence, its most obvious being in reversionary situations, whether over- or under-rented.
- *Full DCF*: The full DCF may also be used as a check on traditional methods. As a valuation method, the DCF is most appropriate for very complex properties such as shopping centres, where there are many variables to be taken into account. Having carried out the DCF, the valuer should check if the resulting initial yield is acceptable and sustainable in market terms. In assessing worth for investment property, the DCF technique is the only acceptable method.

8.2   CAPITAL APPRAISAL TECHNIQUES

Investment appraisal systems need a clear criterion on which to measure the proposals for investment in a project. The appraisal can only deal with money considerations, it cannot deal with qualitative assumptions; thus the criterion is measured on a cash yardstick. The method used must also allow alternative investment projects to be measured against one another. In this section we look at the development of capital appraisal techniques in the business sector for comparison with methods used in property. Just as in the property field, there is a comparison of traditional methods of property valuation with discounted cash flow approaches, and the development of capital appraisal techniques in business mirrors this. The traditional methods in business, however, are more basic than those in the property field. Property valuation methods take into account the concept of discounting income and costs in the future, which illustrate the time value of money in the sense that £1 available today is worth more than £1 in a year's time, even ignoring an inflation effect. This is because if £1 is immediately consumed, the benefit is obtained a year earlier, or the £1 can be invested and earn interest over the year. In property valuation, the traditional Year's Purchase approach takes into account the time value of money whereas, in business valuation, traditional methods ignore this. The two basic approaches discussed first are the payback period method and the rate of return on investment method. The more advanced approaches of discounted cash flow involving net present value (NPV) and internal rate of return (IRR) are dealt with later in this chapter.

Payback period method

This method involves the calculation of the number of years that it takes to pay back the original investment in a project. The important criterion is the length of time: the shorter the period, the better the project (see Example 8.1). Thus, on this basis either project A or B could be chosen and there is no way to distinguish between these in the analysis. Time in this analysis is used in a crude way as it does not take into account the timing of the cash flows, for instance high cash flows in the early years (in projects B and C compared to A), and also the cash flow after the payback period (project C). The advantage of such an approach is in its simplicity and its ability to recognise the time factor, although in a crude way, but no account is taken of the timing of the cash flows, and cash flows occurring after the payback cut-off point, and thus it ignores the overall profitability.

Example 8.1

	PROJECTS		
	A	**B**	**C**
Investment	£10,000	£10,000	£10,000
Cash flow (£)			
Year 1	£1,000	£7,000	£7,000
Year 2	£9,000	£3,000	0
Year 3	£2,000	£2,000	£3,000
Year 4	0	0	£7,000
Total cash inflow	£12,000	£12,000	£17,000
Payback period	2 years	2 years	3 years
Ranking	equal 1	equal 1	3

Rate of return method

This approach expresses a rate of profit as a percentage of the cost of an investment:

$$\frac{\text{Profit}}{\text{Cost}} \times 100\%$$

The cost figure is calculated by the capital employed in the project. A target return is set and if the profitability exceeds this figure, then the project is acceptable. This is a replica of the basic traditional all-risks yield in perpetuity:

$$\frac{\text{Net income}}{\text{Capital value}} \times 100\%$$

Note, however, that the capital value in this context is the price paid or cost, and the yield is an initial yield; this appraisal is thus a form of a market valuation rather than an analysis of the investment. In business finance, the calculation can be done on various bases including profit before tax, profit before interest and tax (PBIT), or profit after tax. Profit figures can be for the first year, the maximum annual figure over the project life, or the average figure over the project life. The latter is usually considered to be the most suitable. Interest is the interest outstanding on debt raised by the company. The capital employed may be shown gross or as an average figure over the life of the asset, deducting each year for depreciation.

Example 8.2: Rate of return

Investment		<u>£8,000</u>
Cash inflows (£)		
Year 1	£4,000	
Year 2	£6,000	
Year 3	£4,000	
Year 4	<u>£2,000</u>	
Total cash inflow		<u>£16,000</u>

Assuming there is no resale or scrap value to the investment, then the original £8,000 is lost at the end of the investment period and the depreciation on the investment if £8,000. Average profit is:

$$\frac{£16,000 - £8,000}{4 \text{ years}} = £2,000\,\text{p.a.}$$

Return on the investment before tax and any interest payment is:

$$\frac{£2,000}{£8,000} \times 100\% = 25\%\,\text{p.a.}$$

Depreciation in the calculation is taken as a straight-line approach for an equal amount of the total depreciation per year. The advantage of this method is that it uses the same criterion related to profitability both for projects and the overall business. The choice of target rate could be the same rate as the firm sets for overall profitability. The disadvantage of using this method is that it again ignores the time value of money. The use of a straight-line approach to depreciation may not realistically reflect the timing of any negative flows. In answer to the deficiencies of the traditional approaches in respect of their inability to take into account the time value of money, business has adopted the discounted cash flow techniques outlined in the following section.

Discounted cash flow techniques

Discounted cash flow (DCF) techniques are an important aid in the evaluation of investment proposals. The overriding advantage of the DCF techniques is that they recognise the time value of money. It should be remembered that DCF analysis is only as accurate as the data that are put into the calculation. Where a rate is used in a DCF calculation, it is more useful as a yardstick than those approaches that use the traditional methods of payback period and return on investment. The evaluation of capital investment techniques has two difficulties. Firstly, costs and revenues arise at different times and this means that they are not directly comparable, this problem is handled by discounted cash flow analysis. The second problem is that the future is uncertain and that forecasted cash flows may not arise as predicted. The discounted cash flow approach appears to give a clear indication of the accept/reject decision for project appraisal and this works well when there is only one project being considered in isolation. In reality, the project will face competition arising from the investor not having sufficient funds to accept all projects indicated as acceptable under the analysis. This is a problem of capital rationing and involves a restriction of choice when resources are limited. The second problem is where two competing projects fulfil the same objective and only one is required. These problems can be investigated by NPV and IRR analysis but the literature shows clearly that the NPV approach is preferred. This analysis concerns individual projects but it may also be necessary to consider investment opportunities as part of a portfolio of investments.

This section has considered the major alternative investment techniques available in the commercial world and the choices that may be made between them. It is also necessary to look at investors and investment companies themselves, because such investigation will bring to light how capital appraisal techniques are used in the corporate sector and how cash flows are generated. There are rules governing the generation of the cash flows, which are related to the accounts of the company. In order to understand the financial affairs of a company, the appraiser must be aware of its financial standing and, if advising on investment in property assets, the appraiser must know about the company's cost of capital. The cost of capital could affect the target discount rate used in discounted cash flow calculations.

8.3 DISCOUNTED CASH FLOW APPROACHES

Comparison of investments is not so simple when the alternatives being considered have varying costs and incomes generated over different periods of time. A technique used to overcome this difficulty is known as 'discounting'; that is, to bring all future amounts, revenue and expenditure, to present-day values using a given rate of interest known as the 'discount rate'; by so doing, a cash flow becomes a 'discounted cash flow' (DCF). DCF is a technique developed by financial appraisers as a tool to assess the overall profitability of a project. Increasingly, the technique is being used by property valuers and analysts, very largely because as financial institutions became more involved in property development and investment, they found the traditional approach of surveyors to be unacceptable on its own. DCF takes into account that incomes and expenditures vary in amounts and in time periods (that is, yearly, monthly, or for alternative periods); in other words, the 'time value' of money is taken into consideration. It can also be used to compare capital projects, but there is some evidence to suggest that in practice simpler methods are used in business (such as payback).

As stated above, the technique is based on calculating the present worth of future sums of money, either income or expenditure (a technique not unknown to valuers who are familiar with using the Present Value of £1 and the Present Value of £1 per annum tables from Parry's Tables, which now include DCF tables (Davidson, 1989). Indeed the traditional investment method estimates the present value of future periodic incomes and therefore 'DCF' is just what valuers have been doing for years. It is true that the traditional method and DCF both find the net present value; however, the important difference lies in the thought processes involved in using the technique and the variation possible to the inputs of the DCF, particularly the rate of interest used.

To produce a DCF, the valuer has at least three forms of discount rate to choose from:

(i) the rate which has to be paid for borrowing capital – the borrowing rate;
(ii) the rate that could be earned if the capital was invested elsewhere – the opportunity rate;
(iii) the rate of return that the investor requires to compensate for the risk involved, the loss of immediate consumption and inflation – the target rate.

In investment appraisal and analysis, it is the target rate which is most commonly used. The level of the target rate could be related to government stock rates, which represents the risk-free rate. To this rate would be added a premium to represent the added risk of the project.

Example 8.3: DCF calculation

Consider an asset A, purchased for £20,000, that will generate the following estimated incomes: year 1, £3,000; year 2, £5,000; year 3, £6,000; year 4, £3,000; year 5, £6,500; year 6, £5,750; year 7, £3,000. In year 4, maintenance cost will be £1,000 and at the end of year 7 the asset will be disposed of for £1,500. If a borrowing rate of 10 per cent per annum is required, the discounted cash flow will be:

Year	Cash flow	Present value of £1 (PV £1 @ 10%)	DCF
0	−£20,000	1	−£20,000
1	3,000	0.909	2,727
2	5,000	0.826	4,130
3	6,000	0.751	4,506
4	3,000		
	−1,000	0.683	1,366
5	6,500	0.621	4,037
6	5,750	0.564	3,243
7	3,000		
	1,500	0.513	2,309
	Net present value @ 10% discount rate		£2,318

The DCF calculation gives a positive answer and thus the asset purchase is worthwhile: at a 10 per cent target threshold it will earn in excess of 10 per cent. At this rate it would provide a £2,318 contribution to profit. The use of a DCF approach when considering a single project is useful, however the technique can be invaluable when alternative investments are to be compared.

There are two forms of DCF used in investment analysis:

- Net Present Value (NPV);
- Internal Rate of Return (IRR).

Net Present Value (NPV)

This is the form of DCF demonstrated above, namely the result of discounting to the present day all sums of money, incoming and outgoing, that the investor incurs.

For single sums, the Present Value of £1 Table can be used, or it can be calculated by using the formula:

$$\frac{1}{(1+i)^n}$$

This will be seen to be the inverse of the Amount of £1, or compound interest formula discussed in earlier chapters. Where the same amount is being received or spent for a series of years, then the Present Value of £1 per annum can be used; this is more familiarly known as the Year's Purchase (YP). It can be seen that it is simply the sum of a series of individual Present Values. For example, using the rate of 8 per cent.

PV £1	1 year @ 8%	0.9259
PV £1	2 years @ 8%	0.8573
PV £1	3 years @ 8%	0.7938
PV £1	4 years @ 8%	0.7350
YP	4 years @ 8%	3.3120

As stated above, the discount rate can be: (i) the borrowing rate; (ii) the opportunity rate; or (iii) the target rate. Whichever form of rate is used, when a positive NPV is obtained then the project will be worthwhile. However, other criteria may need to be considered.

Internal rate of return (IRR)

NPV is most frequently used in investment appraisal for acquisition purposes, but it can also be used for analysis on a trial-and-error basis. More often, though, analysts require to know the actual return on capital to be obtained from an investment. This is the rate generated internally from the income and expenditure incurred, and therefore it is known as the internal rate of return (IRR). It is the discount rate at which the NPV of income equals the NPV of expenditure, or in other words the rate that produces a nil NPV. In the example discussed earlier, if the target rate had been 10 per cent, and it produced a positive NPV, it means that the asset was generating returns about the target rate. A negative NPV would have indicated that the target rate would not have been achieved.

The IRR may be obtained by use of a computer, programmable calculator or Parry's Tables. In the event of none of these being available, then it can be calculated by use of a formula or graph. Both methods require the selection of two discount rates by trial and error, one giving a positive NPV, the other a negative NPV, and then interpolating between the two.

Example 8.4: Calculation of the IRR

Asset A (from Example 8.3):

Year		PV £1 @ 10%	DCF	PV £1 @ 14%	DCF
0	−20,000	1	−£20,000	1	−£20,000
1	3,000	0.909	2,727	0.877	2,631
2	5,000	0.826	4,130	0.769	3,845
3	6,000	0.751	4,506	0.675	4,050
4	3,000				
	−1,000	0.683	1,366	0.592	1,184
5	6,500	0.621	4,037	0.519	3,373
6	5,750	0.564	3,243	0.456	2,622
7	3,000				
	1,500	0.513	2,308	0.400	1,800
		NPV @ 10%	£2,317	NPV @ 14%	−£495

As NPV at 10 per cent is positive and at 14 per cent is negative, and the IRR is the rate at which NPV is zero, then IRR will be at a rate between 10 and 14 per cent. It can be calculated by linear interpolation by using the formula:

$$R_1 + \left[(R_2 - R_1) \times \frac{\text{NPV } R_1}{\text{NPV } R_2 + \text{NPV } R_1} \right]$$

where R_1 = lower rate;   NPV R_1 = NPV lower rate;
       R_2 = higher rate;   NPV R_2 = NPV higher rate;
       in both cases, the + or − signs are ignored. Inserting the data from above:

$$10 + \left[(14 - 10) \times \frac{2,317}{495 + 2,317} \right]$$

IRR = 13.3 per cent

Further examples of discounted cash flow approaches applied to property investments are set out below.

Example 8.5: NPV calculation

The NPV of a project is to be calculated using a purchase price of £10,000. The subsequent cash flows are set out below. Assuming a discount rate of 10 per cent calculate the net present value (NPV).

	Cash flow (£)
Year 1	2,000
Year 2	5,000
Year 3	4,000
Year 4	2,000

Year	Cash flow (£)	PV £1 @ 10%	Present Value (£)
1	2,000	0.909	1,818
2	5,000	0.826	4,130
3	4,000	0.751	3,004
4	2,000	0.683	1,336
			10,318
		less outlay	10,000
		NPV	318

Notes:
1. Cash flows are best estimates and may be net or gross of tax.
2. The discount rate is a target rate, so the NPV is positive, the profit is made and the target is reached and passed.
3. The target rate may be based on: the cost of borrowing; the rate of return on other projects, or the rate on government stock (not equities, as equity yields are low to take into account future growth and may have a risk adjustment).

If the NPV is positive than the investment is worthwhile. If a number of projects are chosen, the one with the highest NPV is chosen, provided the capital outlay is the same. If the capital outlay differs, one needs to calculate the benefit : cost ratio = $\dfrac{\text{discounted PV of total benefits}}{\text{discounted PV of total costs}}$; that with the highest ratio is chosen.

Example 8.6: IRR calculation

Using the cash flows from the previous example to calculate the internal rate of return (IRR).

Year	Cash flow (£)	PV of £1 @ 11%	Present Value (£)	PV £1 @ 12%	Present Value (£)
1	2,000	0.901	1,802	0.893	1,786
2	5,000	0.812	4,060	0.797	3,985
3	4,000	0.731	2,924	0.712	2,848
4	2,000	0.639	1,278	0.636	1,272
			10,064		9,891
		less outlay	10,000		10,000
		NPV	64		(109)

At 11 per cent, a positive NPV is produced and at 12 per cent a negative one, whereas the IRR is that rate which produces a NPV of zero. Therefore the IRR lies in the range of 11–12 per cent. If the NPVs are plotted on a graph against discount rates, a curved line results from which may be read intermediate points to determine the exact IRR. An alternative slightly inaccurate short-cut is to assume a straight-line relationship in which a change in discount rate produces an exactly proportional change in NPV. This is known as linear interpolation, and the IRR may be derived by this method using the following formula as shown previously:

$$R_1 + \left[(R_2 - R_1) \times \frac{\text{NPV } R_1}{\text{NPV } R_2 + \text{NPV } R_1} \right]$$

where R_1 is the lower rate and R_2 is the higher rate, and the signs (+ or –) of the NPV are ignored. Thus in the example, the IRR is:

$$11 + [1 \times (64/173)] = 11.37 \text{ per cent}$$

Property valuation assesses the advantages and disadvantages of an interest in property and expresses them in money terms. DCF techniques facilitate comparisons but IRR techniques do not give the value of the property, only the NPV approach will do this.

Example 8.7: Comparison of YP and PV

Value the income flow for the next four years of £10,000 p.a. payable in arrears from a freehold property if the property is considered an 8 per cent risk.

Net income	£10,000 p.a.
YP for 4 years @ 8%	3.3121
Capital value	£33,121

YP = PV of £1 p.a. = the addition of PV of £1 for each of the years under consideration, thus:

First year's income:
£10,000 × PV £1 in 1 year @ 8% = £10,000 × 0.9259 =   £9,259

Second year's income:
£10,000 × PV £1 in 2 years @ 8% = £10,000 × 0.8573 =   £8,573

Third year's income:
£10,000 × PV £1 in 3 years @ 8% = £10,000 × 0.7938 =   £7,938

Fourth year's income:
£10,000 × PV £1 in 4 years @ 8% = £10,000 × 0.7350 =   £7,350
                                                        £33,120

In this example the income is broken up into a series of cash flows, the YP groups cash flows for a number of periods and the DCF enables annual cash flows to be discerned. The layout usually used in DCF approaches to property calculations is set out in Example 8.8.

Example 8.8: Calculation of net present value (NPV)

End of year	Particulars	Outflow	Inflow	Net flow + or −	PV of £1 @ 12%	Net outflow	Net inflow
0	Purchase price	100,000					
	Purchase costs	8,000		(108,000)	1	108,000	
1	Rent		11,000	11,000	0.8928571		9,821
2	Rent		11,000	11,000	0.7871939		8,769
3	Rent		11,000	11,000	0.7117802		7,830
4	Rent		11,000				
	Sale proceeds		140,000				
	Sale costs	6,000		145,000	0.6355181		92,150
						108,000	118,570
						NPV	10,570

Target rate +12 per cent, NPV @ target rate = £10,570.

Example 8.9: Calculation of the internal rate of return (IRR)

End of year	Particulars	Outflow	Inflow	Net flow + or −	PV of £1 @ 15%	Net outflow	Net inflow
0	Purchase price	100,000					
	Purchase costs	8,000		(108,000)	1	108,000	
1	Rent		11,000	11,000	0.8695652		9,565
2	Rent		11,000	11,000	0.7561437		8,318
3	Rent		11,000	11,000	0.6575162		7,233
4	Rent		11,000				
	Sale proceeds		140,000				
	Sale costs	6,000		145,000	0.6355181		82,904
						108,000	108,020
						NPV	20

Rate at which NPV = 0 is the IRR; here it is approximately 15 per cent, thus the IRR is approximately 15 per cent.

Example 8.10: Investment valuation using DCF (spreadsheet approach)

Investment valuation: DCF						
Purchase price £	50,000,000			Sale price £		72,162,144
Rent passing £	4,000,000			Est. rent on sale £		4,329,729
Initial yield %	8			Est. exit yield %		6
Fees on purchase %	2.75			Fees on sale %		2.75
Rental growth %	2					
Holding period years	5			NPV @ discount rate £		8,236,908
Discount rate %	10			IRR %		13.7843
Rent receivable annually in arrears						

Period	Income	Capital	Fees	Cash flow	DCF	
0	0	−5,000,000	−1,375,000	−51,375,000	−51,375,000	
1	4,080,000			4,080,000	3,709,091	
2	4,161,600			4,161,600	3,439,339	
3	4,244,832			4,244,832	3,189,205	
4	4,329,729			4,329,729	2,957,263	
5	4,416,323	72,162,144	−1,984,459	74,594,008	46,317,010	
				NPV	8,236,908	

SUMMARY OF CHAPTER

- This chapter has discussed a critique of traditional methods.
- It has examined different techniques of capital appraisal.
- It has given examples of the application of discounted cash flow approaches.

REFERENCES AND BIBLIOGRAPHY

Baum, A. and Crosby, N. (1995) *Property Investment Appraisal*, Routledge, London.

Baum, A., Crosby, N. and MacGregor, B. (1996) 'Price formation, mispricing and investment analysis in the property market. A response to "A note on The initial yield revealed: explicit valuations and the future of property investment"', *Journal of Property Valuation and Investment*, Vol. 14, No. 1, pp. 36–49.

Davidson, A. W. (1989) *Parry's Valuation and Investment Tables*, Estates Gazette, London.

French, N. and Ward, C. (1995) 'Valuation and arbitrage', *Journal of Property Research*, Vol. 12, No. 1, Spring, pp. 1–11.

Millington, A. F. (1984) *An Introduction to Property Valuation*, Estates Gazette, London.

Peto, R., French, N. and Bowman, G. (1996) 'Price and worth: Developments in valuation methodology', *Journal of Property Valuation and Investment*, Vol. 14, No. 4, pp. 79–100.

Royal Institution of Chartered Surveyors (RICS) (1994) *President's Working Party on Commercial Property Valuations (Mallinson Report)*, March, RICS, London.

9 Development of the Investment Method

9.1 **Term and reversion**
9.2 **Leasehold property**
9.3 **Hardcore method**
9.4 **Over-rented property**

AIMS AND OBJECTIVES

This chapter extends knowledge of the investment method into the area of term and reversion calculations and leasehold valuations. It examines a different approach to term and reversion calculations by using the hardcore method. Finally, it examines over-rented property as a special case.

Key terms

Term and reversion, reversionary – when a property has been let for some time, the rent will be historic, not at the present market level. At the next rent review, there will be a reversion to the market rent.
Hardcore – the traditional term and reversion values the income in different blocks. The hardcore method suggests a layer or slicing approach that reflects the layers of risk in the income.
Over-rented – this is where an existing historic rent is above the market level, thus at the next rent review there will not be an increase in the rent. The rent will be the same or decrease according to the terms of the lease.

9.1 TERM AND REVERSION

A term and reversion occurs where a freehold is valued subject to a lease that has a rent agreed previously; this rent is therefore historic and does not reflect the full rental value. The usual case in a situation of growth and inflation is that the historic rent would be lower and thus, at the next rent review, the rent would be reviewed to the full rental value. This uplift is referred to as the *reversion* and the period preceding the reversion is the *term*, hence the use of *term rent* and *reversionary rent*. It might be of course, if the market has worsened, that at the next review the rent may, if the lease allows it, go down. This is still a reversion to the full rental value but this over-rented situation may need different techniques to solve it and these approaches are discussed later in the chapter.

Let us look at a complex term and reversion that shows a two-step approach to the reversion.

Example 9.1: Term and reversion

A freehold office building was let 4 years ago on a full repairing and insuring lease for a period of 14 years. The rent agreed for the first 7 years was £5,000 p.a. and for the second 7 years was £6,000 p.a. The current full rental value is £7,000 p.a. Value the freehold interest.

Approach

There are three different rents to be capitalised:

1. £5,000 receivable for 3 years only;
2. £6,000 p.a. receivable for 7 years only but deferred for 3 years; and
3. £7,000 p.a. receivable in perpetuity at the reversion but deferred for 10 years.

Diagram

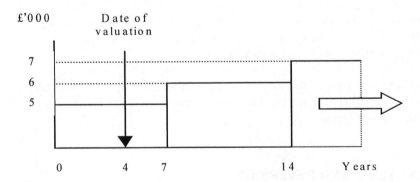

Notes to valuation

1. The rent received under the lease is regarded as being more secure; this is because it carries less risk as it is below the market value, and less risk is reflected in the lower yield.

2. In the second 7-year term, the capital value is obtained by multiplying the rent p.a. by a deferred Year's Purchase (YP for 7 years × PV of £1 for the period of the deferment).
3. The freehold yield is assumed to be the yield of the full rental value, say 6 per cent.

Valuation

Unexpired term: 3 years

Net rent received	£5,000 p.a.
YP for 3 years @ 5%*	2.723 *rent more secure, so 5%
	£13,615

Next 7 years

Net rent received		£6,000
YP for 7 years @ 5%	5.786	
× PV £1 in 3 years @ 5%	0.864	
YP for 7 years @ 5% defrd. 3 years	4.999	
		£29,995

Reversion

Net full rental value	£7,000 p.a.
YP in perp. @ 6% defrd. 10 years	9.307
	£65,149
Capital value	£108,759

In his RICS research, Crosby (1992) suggests that the major criticism of contemporary approaches is that they do not forecast growth and that they subjectively choose a discount rate. He suggests that using implied rental growth rate analysis would reduce the subjectivity. There is a debate between academics over which type of model makes the best use of available evidence: the growth implicit model using comparable transactions to assess an implied growth rate after subjectively choosing a discount rate, or the growth explicit model. The growth explicit model uses the objectively found equivalent yield from comparable transactions and then applies it subjectively to properties to be valued. In Baum and Crosby (1995), the view is that the subjective element in contemporary methods has less effect on the possible range of solutions than the subjective element in conventional approaches, but this is still, however, a minor view in the profession. The market valuation of reversionary freehold property is generally carried out by conventional growth implicit techniques but Crosby's research showed that not all were using the same conventional approach. Crosby, in his paper, indicates that in the future he perceives a demise of the traditional term and reversion approach as reversionary property, valued in a traditional approach, does not use explicit growth. Crosby discovered that of the reversionary techniques used in practice, the traditional term and reversion was not dominant but that the layer approach (also known as the hardcore method) and equivalent yield were also used. There was an even spread across these three approaches (Crosby, 1992). Example 9.2 shows the application of these three methods in a simple valuation.

Example 9.2: The three approaches

A freehold shop is let at an existing rent of £50,000 net. The estimated full rental value (ERV) is estimated at £100,000. The capitalisation rate at full rental value is 5 per cent. There are 3 years left on the lease to run. Calculate the capital value.

Term and reversion

Term rent	£50,000	
YP 3 years @ 4%	2.7751	
		£138,755
Reversion to ERV	£100,000	
YP in perp. @ 5% ×	20.000	
PV £1 in 3 years @ 5%	0.8638	
		£1,727,6.00
Capital value		£1,866,355

Note: The yield on the term is reduced to reflect the security of the income.

Hardcore or layer approach

Term rent	£50,000	
YP in perp. @ 5%	20.000	
		£1,000,000
Reversion to ERV	£100,000	
Less Term rent	£50,000	
Top slice	£50,000	
YP in perp. @ 6% ×	16.667	
PV £1 in 3 years @ 6%	0.8396	
		£699,681
Capital value		£1,699,681

Note: The income stream is split horizontally.

Equivalent yield

Term rent	£50,000	
YP in perp. @ 5%	20.000	
		£1,000,000

Reversion to ERV	£100,000	
Less Hardcore rent	£50,000	
Top slice	£50,000	
YP in perp. @ 5% ×	20.000	
PV £1 in 3 years @ 5%	0.8638	
		£863,800
Capital value		£1,863,800

Note: The income stream may be split vertically as in the traditional term and reversion, or horizontally as in the layer method. As the yield rates for the term and reversion are the same in this calculation, this does not matter.

9.2 LEASEHOLD PROPERTY

Leasehold interests are valued using a dual-rate Year's Purchase, by means of the tables or the equation for the Year's Purchase adjusted for tax (see below). Thus the calculations in this section use two computations: the Present Value of £1, which has been covered earlier, and the dual-rate YP adjusted for tax. A tax rate of 40p in the £1 is used. However, note that tax rates do change and it may be more practical to use a composite rate that is weighted to include lower tax rates on lower bands of income. This is discussed in more detail in Chapter 11 on taxation.

A dual rate is used because it incorporates an annual sinking fund that is used to replace the capital of the asset on the expiration of the lease. Leaseholds depreciate as the term of the lease moves toward its end. The owner of the lease has to put aside capital to replace the asset. It is assumed that the investor will set aside a sum from income to invest and replace the asset at the end of the lease. The annual sinking fund is assumed to attract interest at 3 per cent; this rate is low because it is assumed that the investment that the sinking fund is put into is relatively risk free. Tax is taken into account in the leasehold valuation; the sinking fund is grossed up to allow for tax on the returns, otherwise after tax there will be insufficient in the sinking fund to replace the depreciating asset.

The idea of these adjustments is to put the leasehold on a par with freehold investments so that the yield structure used in the valuation of the freehold can be adjusted and applied to the leasehold interests. Thus, in traditional leasehold valuations, the leasehold yield is derived from the freehold yield and adjusted for tax, and a sinking fund is provided to replace the asset on expiration of the lease. There has been much debate about the relevance of both the sinking fund and the tax adjustment, and critics have suggested that an appropriate approach would be to value without

the sinking fund tax adjustment or even without both. Analysis of yield structure shows that the leasehold yield will, as a rule of thumb, equate to the
freehold yield plus 2 per cent additional risk premium, but a sinking fund
will need to be added to reflect the fact that the lease is a depreciating asset.
The idea of the sinking find is to put the lease back into the same position
as the freehold so that the yield can be compared directly, as seen in the
2 per cent risk addition quoted above. Thus the yield analysis might reveal
the following relationships for leasehold yields:

Details of property type	Additional risk premium	Sinking fund
Prime property	2%	3%
Older property suffering from depreciating and obsolescence in secondary locations or risky property	3–4%	3%

There is an additional risk premium attached to leasehold property
because of a number of reasons:

- there are additional management problems in leaseholds;
- an annual sinking fund needs to be accommodated from the net income
  (say 3 per cent sinking fund net = 5 per cent gross – see later analysis);
- dilapidations need to be accounted for at the end of the lease;
- there could be problems of liquidity, as a lease will be more difficult to
  sell than a freehold because of all the problems indicated here, but also
  because the lease is a wasting asset;
- a lease could be sub-let or given the appropriate lease terms, to further
  sub-letting, thus undermining the security of the investment and adding
  to the management problems while also undermining the possibility of
  immediate total repossession of the property;
- redevelopment or refurbishment potential is less for leasehold and this
  may decrease the value.

The annual sinking fund used in the calculation has to be 'grossed-up'
because the sinking fund will be received net of tax and will be less than
required for reinvestment. This means that a sinking fund of 3 per cent
gross may lose 40 per cent in tax and thus only 1.8 per cent net would be
invested. So the sinking fund has to be 'grossed-up' to ensure the net
amount available after tax is 3 per cent. The calculation is:

Let t = tax rate as a decimal.
Gross rate $\times (1 - t)$ = net rate, and the grossing-up factor is:

$$\text{gross rate} = \text{net rate} \times \frac{1}{(1-t)}$$

If $t = 40$ per cent $= 0.04$ and net rate required for investment is 3 per cent, then the gross rate needed to provide this net rate is:

$$0.03 \times \frac{1}{0.06} = 0.05 = 5\%$$

Net-of-tax calculations are covered in Chapter 11.

Types of leasehold valuation

There are three types of leasehold valuation: rent fixed, rent varying and rent deferred. The freehold could be let to a lessee and in turn let to a sub-lessee. There is an important distinction between the situation where a lessee occupies the premises and where the premises are sub-let. Examples of the two situations are:

- Lessee occupies and pays, say, £100 p.a. to the freeholder. The full rental value in the market is £500 p.a. The valuation in this case is done on the basis of the profit rent; this is the market full rental value *less* the rent paid, in this case £400 p.a.
- The property is sub-let and the lessee does not occupy any of the premises. Assume that the property has been sub-let at £300 p.a. Then in this case the lease is valued on the net income received: the rent received from the sub-lessee *less* the rent payable to the freehold, which is £200 p.a.

Example 9.3: Leasehold valuation

A leasehold interest in a shop is subject to a head rent of £50,000 net. The estimated full rental value (ERV) is estimated at £100,000. The capitalisation rate at full rental value is 5 per cent. There are 3 years left to run on the lease. Calculate the capital value of the leasehold interest.

Dual rate, with sinking fund tax adjusted

ERV	£100,000 p.a.	
Less Head rent	£50,000 p.a.	
Profit rent	£50,000 p.a.	
YP 3 years @ 6% + 3% (40p tax)	1.6688	
Capital value		£83,440

Note: The criticisms of this approach relate to: how the leasehold rate is assessed from the freehold; the tax rate is an individual calculation, and not a market one; and the remuneration rate used, at 3 per cent, is low.

As an alternative, there is an argument to use a single rate:

Single rate

ERV	£100,000 p.a.	
Less Head rent	£50,000 p.a.	
Profit rent	£50,000 p.a.	
YP 3 years @ 6%	2.6730	
Capital value		£133,650

Profit rent

The profit rent per annum is the full rental value *less* the rent paid by an occupying lessee or a sub-lessee. Where a profit rent exists, the occupier has a saving on the annual expenses because the rent payment is less than the full rental value. This situation occurs because the lessee or sub-lessee has been in occupation for a period of time and the rent has not been reviewed recently, or a premium may have been paid at the commencement or during the period of the lease. If the occupier wishes to sell the lease or sub-lease, the valuation will capitalise the profit rent to arrive at a capital value.

Example 9.4: Leasehold valuation

A shop is let on a full repairing and insuring lease; the lease has 12 years unexpired. The rent being paid is £1,200 p.a. The net rental value is £1,500 p.a. Assume a yield of 7 per cent and a tax liability of 40p in the £. Value the leasehold interest. (In this case we are using a sinking fund of 2.5 per cent.)

Valuation

Net full rental value	£1,500	
less Rent paid	£1,200	
Profit rent		£300
YP for 12 years @ 7% and 2.5% (tax 40p in £)		5.241
Capital value		£1,572

Notes to valuation

1. The lessee is in occupation, so the valuation is to profit rent.
2. The annual sinking fund is used to replace the depreciating leasehold asset to put it on the same comparative footing as a freehold valuation. The freehold yield here might therefore be, say, 6 per cent with 1 per cent added for leasehold risks.

3. If the sinking fund is taxed there will not be enough to put away to replace the asset at the end of its life. The tax adjustment allows for more sinking fund to be put away to pay the tax on the 2.5 per cent interest. So at a tax rate of 40p the net income from £1 will only be 60p. So the sinking fund rate is grossed-up:

$$£1 \times \frac{100}{100 - t} = £1 \times \frac{100}{60} = £1.67$$

Thus the calculation allows for £1.67 to be put aside instead of £1, and the net result after tax at 40 per cent will be the £1 we need to invest.

To get to a profit rent, the comparison requires the full market rental and the rent paid to be on the same terms. It is a comparison of like with like. So if the full rental value estimate used is on the basis of fully repairing and insuring terms, so must the rent being paid; if not, then adjustments must be made. Table 9.1 shows the comparison of adjustments for different repair and insurance responsibilities. For this example we will assume a full rental value of £1,000 p.a. with external repairs costing £100 p.a., internal repairs £50 p.a., insurance £25 p.a. and management fee of £100 which is a cost of organising the activities.

Example 9.5: Internal repairing lease

A property is let on an internal repairing lease at £1,000 p.a. The net rack rent is £1,200 p.a. Calculate the profit rent p.a.

Approach

If the tenant were only responsible for internal repairs, then the tenant would expect to pay more than £1,200 p.a. That is, £1,200 plus external repairs and insurance to put the rack rent on the same basis.

Calculation

Net full rental value	£1,200 p.a.
Add: external repairs @ 10% net rent	£120 p.a.
insurance @ 2.5% net rent	£30 p.a.
Adjusted full rental value	£1,350 p.a.
Profit rent is:	
Adjusted full rental value	£1,350 p.a.
Less: rent paid p.a.	£1,000 p.a.
Profit rent p.a.	£350 p.a.

Table 9.1 Calculation of rental given a range of outgoings

Adjustments to be made	Tenant's responsibility			
	All repairs and insurance (full repairing and insuring lease)	No responsibility for repairs and insurance	Responsible for internal repairs and insurance	Responsible for insurance only
Full rental value	£1,000	£1,275	£1,200	£1,250
Cost of external repairs p.a.	£100	Nil	Nil	Nil
Cost of internal repairs p.a.	£50	Nil	£50	Nil
Cost of insurance p.a.	£25	Nil	£25	£25
Cost of management	£100	Nil	Nil	Nil
Total cost to tenant of rent, repairs insurance and management charges	£1,275	£1,275	£1,275	£1,275

Premiums

A premium is a sum of money that is paid by the lessee at the commencement of the lease or during the lease in return for a reduction in rent. The lessee, through the premium, purchases part of the profit rent and the landlord capitalises a part of the future income due (takes a capital sum in place of a portion of the annual rental). Thus in this situation the remaining rental, being lower than the rental expected, would be more secure and this would have an impact on the yield rate applied. The premium paid is thus the capitalisation of all or part of the profit rent. This situation will only happen if the landlord is prepared to negotiate on such a position. Note that leases are usually 25 years with 5-year reviews, but pressure is now being put on landlords to reduce the terms for flexibility. In the examples here, a range of lease types is used to provide a variety of calculations.

Example 9.6: Calculation of premium

A landlord has granted a 14-year lease of a shop, the net full rental value being £1,500 p.a. The lessee has agreed to pay £1,000 p.a. and wants the remainder capitalised as a premium and paid up-front. Calculate the premium. Assume a leasehold yield of 7 per cent and a tax liability of 40 per cent.

Net full rental value p.a.	£1,500
Less Rent to be paid p.a.	£1,000
Profit rent p.a.	£500
YP 14 yrs @ 7% and 2.5% (tax 40%)	5.852
Premium	£2,926

Working backward in the calculation, if a premium of £2,926 is offered, divide this by the YP 14 yrs @ 7% and 2.5% net (tax 40%) to get the profit rent:

$$\text{Reduction in rent p.a.} = \frac{\text{premium}}{\text{YP for the term of the lease}} = \text{annual equivalent}$$

Graphically the principle is (assuming a 7-year lease @ £1,000 p.a. net full rental value):

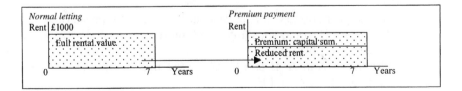

Example 9.7: Premium

A shop is let on a 14-year lease on FRI terms; the net full rental value is £1,400 p.a. The tenant has agreed to pay a premium of £4,000 at the commencement of the lease. Calculate the annual rent to be paid. Assume a yield of 8 per cent and a tax liability of 40 per cent.

Premium is £4,000.

$$\begin{array}{l}\text{Annual equivalent} \\ \text{of premium}\end{array} = \frac{£4,000}{\text{YP for 14 years @ 8\% and 2.5\% net (tax at 40\%)}}$$

$$= \frac{£4,000}{5.528} = £724 \text{ p.a.}$$

= reduction in rent or profit rent

In this situation the rent to be paid can be calculated from:

Net full rental value	£1,400 p.a.
Less Annual equivalent of premium	£724 p.a.
Equals the reduced rent payable	£626 p.a.

Graphically:

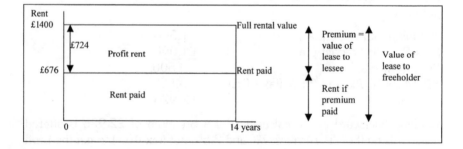

Example 9.8: Freehold, leasehold, sub-leasehold and marriage value

A shop is owned freehold by A and let to B. There are 13 years unexpired on the lease. B pays rates and does internal repairs only. (So A pays for fire insurance and does external repairs.) The rent payable under the lease is £1,000 p.a.

B sub-let the property to C for six years at £15,000 p.a. plus a premium of £1,000. C pays B's outgoings (rates and internal repairs). The rental at full rental value is £2,500 p.a.

Value the interests in A, B and C. Show the maximum amount C will pay for the interests of A and B.

Valuation of freehold (A's interest)

1. Assume freehold yield on full rental terms is 7 per cent.
2. Rent needs to be adjusted to net income because external repairs and insurance have to be paid for.

Diagram

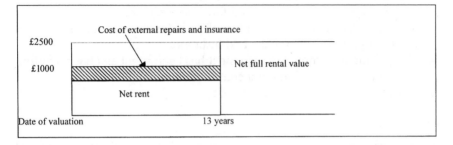

Method

- Value the first block, deduct an allowance from the rent for repairs and insurance, and adjust the yield from the yield at full rental value.
- Value the second block in perpetuity at the yield given (assumes FRI lease on reversion).

Freehold valuation

A's interest

Assumptions: Yield on reversion   7 per cent
               Yield on term   6 per cent
               Income is gross: percentage deduction for external repairs and insurance, say 7.5 per cent

Term:	£	
Rent received p.a.	1,000	
less Allowance for external repairs and insurance @ 7.5 per cent of full rental value (£2,500)	187	
Net income per annum	813	
YP 13 years @ 6%	8.853	
Capital value of term		7,197
Reversion:		
Net full rental value p.a.	2,500	
YP in perpetuity deferred 13 years @ 7%	5.928	
Capital value of reversion		14.820
Capital value of freehold		£22,017

Valuation of B's leasehold interest

Assumptions:

1. B is not in possession, so valuation is on the basis of net income: rent received *less* rent paid.
2. The leasehold yield at rack rent is higher than the freehold yield @ 7 per cent. The yield for the first term is lower than the second term because it is a lower income and thus more secure.
3. The full rental value needs to be adjusted for the fact that the tenant does not pay external repairs and insurance.
4. The premium is ignored, so assume it has been spent and has no further effect on existing and future income.
5. Tax rate assumed to be 40 per cent.

Diagram

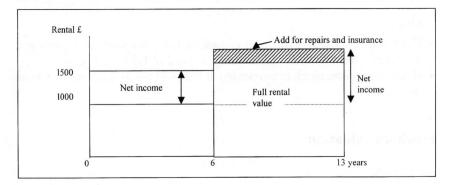

Leasehold valuation

B's interest

First 6 years:	£
Rent received p.a.	1,500
less Rent paid	1,000
Net income per annum	500
YP 6 years @ 7% + 2.5% net (40% tax)	3.022
Capital value of term	1,511

Next 7 years:
Reversion to adjusted full rental value, i.e. £2,500 *plus* allowance

for repairs and insurance (£2,500 + £187)	2,687
less Rent paid	1,000
Net income per annum	1,687

YP 7 years @ 8% + 2.5% net (40% tax)		3.324
PV £1 in 6 years @ 8%	×	0.63
		2.094
Capital value of second term		3,532
Total capital value		£5,043

Valuation of C's interest (Sub-leasehold) – diagram

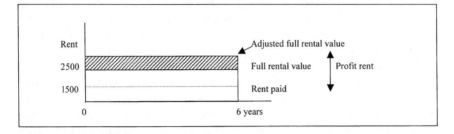

Sub-leasehold valuation

Adjusted full rental value	2,687
less Rent paid	1,500
Profit rent p.a.	1,187
YP 6 years @ 8.5% + 2.5% net (40% tax)	2.891
Capital value	£3,432

Marriage valuation

If C purchased the interests of B and A, C would own the freehold worth:

Freehold in possession

Net rack rental	2,500	
YP in perp. @ 7%	14.286	
Capital value		35,715
less Value of C's existing interest		3,450
Difference is maximum C would pay		£32,265

Other investors would buy the interests of A and B separately, i.e.

A	£22,017
B	£5,043
Total	£27,060

So C could outbid them because of the marriage of the interests.

9.3   HARDCORE METHOD

The hardcore method is now being used widely in practice. There are advantages and disadvantages in respect of this method. The method has advantages in the sense that it can be used to isolate the increase in rental value on rent review and reversion. It can thus treat this top slice income in a different way. In a volatile market, it can try to estimate the risk of the top slice. It also appears to be applicable in situations where a valuation may be based on turnover rents, where there is a base or core rent calculated and to which is added an additional slice based on the actual turnover of the company operating from the property. On the other hand, its disadvantages are really that it invokes an artificial division of the income. The security of the reversionary income is not divisible; if the tenants default, then they default in the payment of the whole income, not just the top slice. It is also difficult to value using comparables from the market, as the comparables would only provide an equivalent yield on the basis of which two unknown quantities, the hardcore yield and the marginal yield, need to be calculated. In using comparable evidence from a conventional term and reversion valuation, there can be great differences in the calculation where the term income is substantially below the current full market rental value. However, the system may be useful in situations similar to the market of the late 1980s and 1990s, in that any downturn in the market can mean a reduction of rental at the next rent review. Therefore the ability to layer the income into different slices can mean that the top slice can be treated more appropriately, with its inherent risk possibly being ignored completely in some cases. It could also be used as a valuation method where there are contractual agreements to put the income at review above a market rental value. This means that the increase at review is very risky because it makes a tenant uncompetitive and reluctant to pay the rent. Criticisms of overvaluation of the core income in the hardcore method and undervaluation of the marginal income really arise because of the use of an inappropriate schedule of discount rates based on conventional term and reversion yields rather than direct comparables. The high risk of the top slice rental relative to the hardcore rent needs to be taken into account.

Valuation of reversionary investments

There are two different approaches to valuing reversionary investments:

- *Term and reversion*: a block income approach.
- *Hardcore method*: a layer approach.

(Note that a reversionary investment is where a property is let at less than the estimated rental value (ERV) but there is a likelihood of a rent review or re-letting at the full rental value.)

Block income approach

Term: capitalise the present rent till reversion.
Reversion: capitalise full rental value in perpetuity.
Total: add term and reversion.

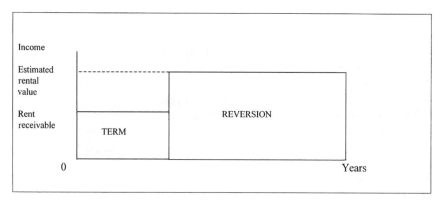

Conventional approach

Layer approach

Hardcore: capitalise the present rent in perpetuity.
Incremental rent: capitalise top slice from reversion in perpetuity.
Total: add hardcore and incremental rent.

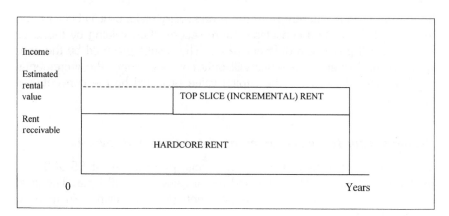

Hardcore (layer) approach

If term and reversion are at the same yield, then you can apply this rate to the layer method and get the same result:

Example 9.9: Hardcore, same yields term and reversion

Value the freehold interest in a commercial premises let at £5,000 p.a. for the next 3 years. The estimated rental value is £8,000 p.a. The yield at the estimated rental value is 8 per cent.

Conventional approach

Term		
Rent received	£5,000 p.a.	
YP 3 yrs @ 8%	2.577	
		£12,885
Reversion to ERV	£8,000 p.a.	
YP in perp. @ 8% defrd. 3 yrs	9.923	
		£79,384
Capital value		£92,269

Layer approach

Hardcore		
Hardcore rent received	£5,000 p.a.	
YP in perp. @ 8%	12.5	
		£62,500
Incremental rent	£3,000 p.a.	
YP in perp. @ 8% defrd. 3 yrs	9.923	
		£29,769
Capital value		£92,269

If the term yield is different from the reversionary yield, usually because the term rate is lower and considered more secure, then valuing by the layer approach will produce a different result. The results provided by the conventional and layer approaches will only coincide where the incremental yield is adjusted to match the capital value provided by the conventional approach.

Example 9.10: Hardcore, different yields term and reversion

Value the freehold interest in a commercial premises let at £5,000 p.a. for the next 3 years. The estimated rental value is £8,000 p.a. The yield at the estimated rental value is 8 per cent. (Assume term yield to be 6 per cent.)

Conventional approach

Term

Rent received	£5,000 p.a.	
YP 3yrs @ 6%	2.673	
		£13,365
Reversion to ERV	£8,000 p.a.	
YP in perp. @ 8% defrd. 3yrs	9.923	
		£79,384
	Capital value	£92,649

Layer approach

Method:

1. *Determine yield on hardcore rent.* The hardcore rent = term rent, therefore use term yield, i.e. 6 per cent.
2. *Determine yield on increment* to arrive at the same valuation as the conventional method:

$$\text{Yield on increment} = \frac{\text{Incremental income}}{\text{Capital value of incremental income}}$$

Incremental income = estimated rental value − term rent = £8,000 − £5,000 = £3,000

Capital value of incremental income = capital value of estimated rental value in perpetuity *minus* the capital value of the hardcore rent in perpetuity, thus:

Estimated rental value	£8,000 p.a.	
YP in perp. @ 8%	12.5	
		£100,000
less Hardcore (term) rent	£5,000 p.a.	
YP in perp. @ 6%	16.666	
	£83,330	
Capital value of incremental income		£16,670

$$\text{Yield on increment} = \frac{£3,000}{£16,670} \times 100\% = 18\%$$

3. *Valuation*

Hardcore rent received	£5,000 p.a.	
YP in perp. @ 6%	16.666	
		£83,330
Incremental rent	£3,000 p.a.	

YP in perp. @ 18% defrd. 3 yrs.   3.381

	£10,143
Capital value	£93,473

(Compare with traditional approach = £92,649)

Example 9.11: Hardcore valuation (spreadsheet approach)

Value the freehold interest in a commercial premises let at £5,000 p.a. for the next 2 years.

The estimated rental value is £10,000 p.a. The yield at ERV is 10 per cent. Assume term yield is 8 per cent.

Data:	Rent received	£	5,000 p.a.
	ERV		10,000 p.a.
	Years to review		2
	Yield @ ERV		10.00%
	Term yield		8.00%

Conventional approach

Term	£	£
Rent received	5,000 p.a.	
YP yrs. 2 @ 8.00%	1.783	
		8,916
Reversion to ERV	10,000	
YP perp. @ 10.00% defrd. 2 years	8.264	
		82,645
Capital value		£91,561

Layer approach

Hardcore yield = term yield = 8.00%

$$\text{Yield on increment} = \frac{\text{Incremental income}}{\text{Capital value of incremental income}}$$

Incremental income = estimated rental value − term rent
= £10,000 − £5,000 = £5,000

CV of incremental income = CV ERV in perp. − CV hardcore rent in perp.

Estimated rental value	£	10,000 p.a.
YP in perp. @ 10%		10.000
		100,000

less

Hardcore (term) rent	£	5,000 p.a.

YP in perp. @ 8%		12.500	
			62,500
Capital value of incremental income			£37,500

$$\text{Yield on increment} = \frac{5,000}{37,5000} \times 100\% = 13.33\%$$

Hardcore valuation

Hardcore rent received	£	5,000 p.a.		
YP in perp. @ 8%		12.500		
			62,500	
Incremental rent	£	5,000 p.a.		
YP perp. @ 13.33% defrd. 2 years		5.839		
			29,196	
	Capital value		£91,696	

9.4 OVER-RENTED PROPERTY

The layer approach used above can also deal with situations where properties are over-rented; that is, where the property is let at a rental value higher than the estimated rental value and thus where the rental will fall at the next review. The over-rented layer of rent (the overage) is thus treated differently from the core which represents the estimated rental value; see Example 9.12.

Example 9.12: Over-rented – hardcore or layer approach

A freehold shop is let at an existing rent of £100,000 net. The estimated full rental value (ERV) is estimated at £50,000. The capitalisation rate at full rental value is 5 per cent. The lease has 10 years to run with upward only rent reviews. Calculate the capital value of the freehold.

Core rent		
ERV	£50,000	
YP in perp. @ 5%	20.000	
		£1,000,000
Top slice		
Rent passing	£100,000	
Less ERV	£50,000	
Overage	£50,000	
YP 10 years @ 10%	6.1146	

	£305,730
Capital value	£1,305,730

Notes: The calculation assumes that the full rental value will be less than the rent passing for the duration of the lease and beyond. By applying implied growth to the rental level, the precise time can be found when the ERV has grown to the same level as the rent passing. Assuming this is in 5 years' time, then the overage can only be valued for the 5-year period. The problem of this method is that the rental growth is exaggerated in the valuation of the core income and in the overage. This can be overcome by valuing as a term and reversion for the 10-year period; see Example 9.13.

Example 9.13: Over-rented – term and reversion

Term rent		£100,000
YP 10 years @ 10%		6.1146
		£611,460
Reversion to ERV		£50,000
YP in perp. @ 5% ×	20.000	
PV £1 in 10 years @ 5%	0.6139	
	12.278	
		£613,900
Capital value		£1,225,360

SUMMARY OF CHAPTER

This chapter has developed the investment method of valuation and applied it to:

* The term and reversion.
* Leasehold property.
* The hardcore method.
* Over-rented property.

REFERENCES AND BIBLIOGRAPHY

Baum, A. and Crosby, N. (1995) *Property Investment Appraisal*, Routledge, London.

Crosby, N. (1991) 'Over-rented freehold investment property valuation', *Journal of Property Valuation and Investment*, Vol. 10, No. 2, pp.517–24.

Crosby, N. (1992) *Reversionary Freeholds; UK Market Valuation Practice*, Research Paper, RICS, London.

Crosby, N. and Goodchild, R. (1992) 'Reversionary freeholds: problems with over-renting', *Journal of Property Valuation and Investment*, Vol. 11, No. 1, pp.67–81.

10 Yields and Interest Rates

10.1 Interest rates, risk and inflation
10.2 The equivalent yield
10.3 The equated yield
10.4 The implied growth rate

AIMS AND OBJECTIVES

This chapter aims to investigate aspects of interest rates and yields and to break these down into the components of liquidity, inflation and risk. It then goes on to use these concepts in the analysis of equivalent and equated yields and the implied growth rate.

Key terms

The analysis of yields:
Base case = IRR
IRR on full rental value = *the all-risk yield*
IRR in a term and reversion = *equivalent yield*
IRR with growth of income = *equated yield*
Implied growth rate – the all-risks yield has implied growth; by inputting a target rate (the equated yield), the growth rate of income can be imputed.

10.1 INTEREST RATES, RISK AND INFLATION

Risk and inflation are important matters for property investors. The yield used by property investors is an interest rate return, and interest rates are calculated on the basis of three elements. The components of the interest rate or yield consist of:

• compensation for the time preference of money;
• an inflation allowance to maintain the real value of the return;
• an element for risk-taking.

Time preference element

This element exists as a compensation to the investor who now cannot spend the investment immediately but will need to wait until the investment is sold. The compensation stems from the view that individuals prefer to have money available now rather than later. The money could thus be consumed or invested, allowing for immediate satisfaction from the consumables of income from the investment. The interest rate needs to entice individuals to part with their money and delay consumption. This could be thought of as a liquidity element.

Inflation allowance

An inflation allowance used in interest rates should be the reflection of the investor's anticipation of the inflation rate, and this may differ from economic assumptions held by the government and other investors. At this point, the analysis can show the relationship between market rates of interest, which are inclusive of inflation, and real rates of interest. This is given by the equation:

(1 + real rate of interest) × (1 + rate of general inflation)
= (1 + market rate of interest)

or $$(1 + i) \times (1 + g) = (1 + e)$$ **(equation 10.1)**

so $$i = \frac{(1+e)}{(1+g)} - 1$$

where i is the real rate of interest, g is the rate of general inflation and e is the market rate of interest, all as decimals. As an example, if the rental growth (at market rate = e) is 6 per cent and the rate of inflation (g) is 7 per cent, the real rate of growth can be seen to be negative, around –1 per cent, or more precisely:

$$i = \frac{(1+0.06)}{(1+0.07)} - 1 = -0.0093$$

Risk premium

This is the addition to the risk-free interest rate to take into account the risk of the investment. There is a trade-off between risk and reward; for additional risk, a greater reward is expected by the investor and vice versa. This relationship is represented diagrammatically by Figure 10.1. The capital market line, risk, reward and the relationships between them are discussed in detail later in the book. By dividing the real rate of interest into its elements of time preference and the risk premium, the element of the risk premium can be exposed. Thus:

$$(1 + i) = (1 + d)(1 + r) \qquad \textbf{(equation 10.2)}$$

Inserting into equation 10.1 above: $(1 + d)(1 + r)(1 + g) = (1 + e)$

Here d and r are the time preference and risk elements respectively, and rearranging:

$$e = (1 + g)(1 + d)(1 + r) - 1$$

so if the risk element were taken out, a risk-free return (RFR) would be:

$$RFR = (1 + i)(1 + d) - 1$$

and $$e = (1 + RFR)(1 + r) - 1$$

Multiplying out:

$$e = 1 + r + RFR + rRFR - 1$$

But $rRFR$ will be small and an approximation is $e = RFR + r$; thus the market rate of interest is equal to the risk-free rate plus the risk premium attached by the market.

Property as an inflation hedge

Is property a good hedge against inflation? Matysiak *et al.* (1995) used a multivariate analysis of long-term total returns and inflation data over the period 1963–93. They found no evidence that property returns provide a

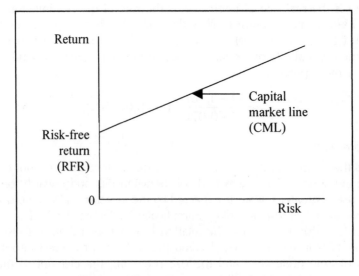

Figure 10.1   *The capital market line*

hedge on an annual basis against expected or unexpected components of inflation. Barkham *et al.* (1995) found a long-term relationship between property and inflation in the short and long term, but that the adjustment of property to inflation or vice versa is very weak or slow. They used cointegration techniques and commented that their contribution to the debate is to bring back a longer-term perspective to the argument of the need to supplement property investment in portfolios. Cointegration techniques have been developed to deal with time series where the variables under consideration are non-stationary, and therefore this method can be used to test a statistical long-term relationship between property returns and inflation. Nevertheless, the findings from the study of Barkham *et al.* showed that property is not a consistent hedge over the time periods examined.

10.2 THE EQUIVALENT YIELD

Reversionary investments can be valued by the traditional or the hardcore method. Investors, though, may require to know the overall yield of a reversionary investment. For instance, if the term yield is 6 per cent and the reversionary yield is 8 per cent, what is the overall yield?

If rates on the term and reversion are the same, then the equivalent yield is the same.

Example 10.1: The equivalent yield

A shop is let at £5,000 p.a. net. The estimated rental value (ERV) is £20,000 p.a. There are 3 years unexpired on the lease. Calculate the equivalent yield.

Term and reversion

Term					£	£
Rent received					5,000	
YP	3 yrs @		5%		2.7237	
						13,616
Reversion						
Estimated rental value (ERV)					20,000	
YP in perp. deferred	3 yrs @		7%	11.6614		
						233,228
Capital value						£246,844

Calculation of the equivalent yield:

1. by formula;
2. by discounted cash flow.

Solution by formula

$$\text{Equivalent yield} = \frac{(\text{Present income} + \text{Annual equivalent of gain}^*)}{\text{Capital value}} \times 100\%$$

Know: Present income: £5,000 p.a.
         Capital value (from term and reversion calculation): £246,844

*Need to find**

$$\text{Annual equivalent of gain} = \frac{\text{Gain on reversion}^\dagger \times \text{PV £1 for term}}{\text{YP for term}}$$

† *Gain on reversion* = Value of reversion − Capital value

Calculation

Value on reversion:	£
Estimated rental value	20,000
YP in perp. @ 7%	14.286
	285,714

Therefore gain on reversion = 285,714 − 246,844 = £38,780

Annual equivalent

$$\text{of gain} = \frac{£38,870 \times \text{PV £1 @ 6.50\%}^* \text{ in 3 yrs}}{\text{YP 3 yrs @ 6.50\%}^*}$$

*Rate is a guess at

$$\text{the equivalent yield} = \frac{£38,870 \times 0.8278}{2.6485} = \underline{\underline{£12,150}}$$

$$\text{Equivalent yield} = \frac{£5,000 + £12,150}{£246,844} = 6.95\%$$

* Recalculate rate until it accords with the equivalent yield, e.g.

$$\text{Annual equivalent of gain} = \frac{£38,870 \times \text{PV £1 @ 6.93\%}^* \text{ in 3 yrs}}{\text{YP 3 yrs 6.93\%}^*}$$

$$\text{* Rate is a guess at the equivalent yield} = \frac{£38,870 \times 0.8179}{2.6277} = £12,099$$

$$\text{Equivalent yield} = \frac{£5,000 + £12,099}{£246,844} = 6.93\%$$

Diagram to show concept

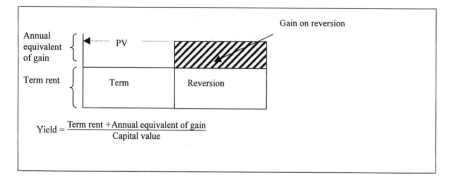

Solution by DCF

Years	Cash flow	YP 3 yrs @ 6%	PV £1 in 3 yrs @ 6%	PV cash flow	YP 3 yrs @ 7%	PV £1 in 3 yrs @ 7%	PV cash flow
1–3	5,000	2.6730		13,365	2.6243		13,122
3 on	285,714		0.8396	239,890		0.8163	233,228
				253,256			246,349
		less Price paid		−246,844	*less* Price paid		−246,844
			NPV	6,412		NPV	−495

By linear interpolation:
$$\text{IRR} = 6\% + \frac{6,412}{6,412 + 495} = 6\% + 0.9284$$

Equivalent yield (IRR) = 6.93%

This approach is the same as used for the Gross Redemption Yield, which is quoted on government securities that bear an income and a capital sum on redemption.

10.3 THE EQUATED YIELD

Growth can be built into DCF cash flows so that the IRR of the calculation represents the equated yield, that is the yield with an explicit growth or inflation rate. The NPV that arises from such a calculation thus will take into account the growth in rental levels; this is shown in the calculation of the equated yield set out below.

The technique of equated yield analysis is as follows:

(i) Assume a growth rate in the rental per annum. Apply this to the original income using the Amount of £1.
(ii) Insert the income with growth into the DCF analysis; once the IRR has been found, this is the equated yield.

Example 10.2: Calculation of equated yield

A freehold investment has been purchased for £100,000; it has a rack rental value of £5,000 p.a. It is let on a lease for 25 years with 5-year rent reviews. Assuming rental growth of 10 per cent p.a., determine the equated yield. The layout used below is a possible presentation of the calculation, if a computer spreadsheet were to be used.

Capital value	£100,000	
Initial rent	£5,000 p.a.	
Initial yield/YP	5%	20 YP
Trial equated yields	14%	15%
Rent review frequency	5 yearly	
Growth rate p.a.	10% compound	
YP for the review period at the trial rate	3.43081	3.352155

(These YPs are based on the YP for 5 years, the review period, at the trial rates of 14 per cent and 15 per cent as above.)

Period (years)	Amt £1 @ 10%	Cash flow	PV £1 @ 14%	Deferred YP	PV of slice
0	n/a	−100,000	n/a		−100,000
1–5	n/a	5,000	n/a	3.433081	17,165
6–10	1.610510	8,053	0.5193687	1.783035	14,358
11–15	2.593742	12,969	0.2697438	0.9260523	12,010
16–20	4.177248	20,886	0.1400965	0.4809626	10,046
21–25	6.727500	33,637	0.0727617	0.2497969	8,403
26–30	10.83471	54,174	0.0377902	0.1297367	7,028
31–perp.	17.44940	87,247	0.0196270	0.3925405	34,248
				Net present value	3,257

Period (years)	Amt £1 @ 10%	Cash flow	PV £1 @ 14%	Deferred YP	PV of slice
0	n/a	−100,000	n/a		−100,000
1–5	n/a	5,000	n/a	3.352155	16,761
6–10	1.610510	8,053	0.4971767	1.666614	13,420
11–15	2.593742	12,969	0.2471847	0.8286015	10,746
16–20	4.177248	20,886	0.1228945	0.4119614	8,604
21–25	6.727500	33,637	0.0611003	0.2048176	6,890
26–30	10.83471	54,174	0.0303776	0.1018306	5,517
31–perp.	17.44940	87,247	0.0151031	0.3020611	26,354
				Net present value	−11,709

$$\text{IRR} = 14 + \left(1 \times \frac{3,257}{14,966}\right) = 14.22\%$$

Notes to the calculation:

1. Because the rent review period is for 5 years, the calculation deals with the cash flows in slices of 5 years as the income cannot change within the 5-year period.
2. The cash flows for each period have been inflated by the amount of £1 at the growth rate of 10 per cent to the beginning of each period, showing the rent with growth at each review.
3. The deferral rate is calculated for each cash flow period for each trial rate (PV £1 for deferred period at 14 and 15 per cent). This is multiplied by the PV £1 column to give the deferred YP.
4. The period cash flow is valued by capitalising at the trial rates for the 5-year period (YP 5 years at 14 and 15 per cent). This is multiplied by the PV £1 column to give the deferred YP.
5. The deferred YP at the trial rates is multiplied by the inflated cash flow to give the value of the deferred slice. The values of the deferred slices are added together to give the net present value.
6. To calculate the equated yield which is the IRR of the calculation, we need to arrive at a positive and negative NPV, and interpolate between them to obtain the point where the NPV = 0; this is then the yield, which is the IRR.
7. The calculation could go on indefinitely, but cash flows after 30 years because of the deferral factor make much less difference to the calculation; after this, no growth is added to the income and thus the initial yield is used for the trial rates. In this case, the initial yield is 5 per cent and the final deferred YP is YP in perpetuity @ 5 per cent deferred 30 years. In view of the problems of predicting growth over the longer period, it may be more desirable to restrict the analysis to 20 years.

An alternative way of arriving at the equated yield is to use the equation that underpins the calculation. The equated yield equation is:

$$I = E - E\left[\frac{(1+G)^n - 1}{(1+E)^n - 1}\right]$$

where I is the initial or all-risks yield $= \dfrac{\text{rack rent}}{\text{purchase price}}$ when the property is freehold or let at the rack rent or full rental value – the yield is expressed as a decimal in the equation, not a percentage;

E is the equated yield as a decimal;
G is the annual growth rate in rental income compounded as a decimal; and
n is the rent review period in years.

This equation, which lies behind the DCF calculation used above, can be used directly to compute the growth rate, and this is shown in Example 10.3, the calculation to find the implied growth rate.

10.4   THE IMPLIED GROWTH RATE

There are a number of ways of doing this, as shown in Example 10.3.

Example 10.3: The implied growth rate

A freehold shop is let on a 25-year lease with 5-year reviews at the full rental value of £25,000. The property has been sold for £500,000. What is the implied rental growth rate?

Capitalisation rate $(k) = \dfrac{£25,000}{£500,000} = 0.05 = 5$ per cent

Target rate of return (assumed) $(e) = 15$ per cent
Rent review period $(t) = 5$ years
Implied annual growth rate (g) is calculated from the formula (this is the same formula as the above but the terms used are different; there are two different sources and it is up to the reader which is chosen):

$$k = e - \frac{e\left[(1+g)^t - 1\right]}{(1+e)^t - 1}$$

so

$$0.05 = 0.15 - \frac{0.15\left[(1+g)^5 - 1\right]}{(1+0.15)^5 - 1}$$

and $g = 0.1085 = 10.85$ per cent

An alternative formula on the same basis is:

$$(1+g)^t = \frac{\text{YP perp.} @ k - \text{YP } t \text{ years } @ e}{\text{YP perp.} @ k \times \text{PV } t \text{ years } @ e}$$

The analysis of growth from example 10.3 is used in example 10.4.

Example 10.4: Shortened cash flow model

Shortened cash flow model (spreadsheet layout)					
Freehold shop					
Lease	25	years	5	year reviews	
Existing year of lease			0		
Years to review			5		
Equated yield			15.00%		
Market capitalisation			5.00%		
Net rental value	£		100,000	p.a.	
Implied rate of growth			10.86%		
Period	Amt £1 @	Cash	PV £1 @	Deferred	PV of
(years)	10.86%	flow	15.00%	YP	slice
0–5	1	100,000	1	3.352155	335,216
6–10	1.674238	167,424	0.497177	1.666614	279,031
11–15	2.803073	280,307	0.247185	0.828601	232,263
16–20	4.693012	469,301	0.122894	0.411961	193,334
21–25	7.85722	785,722	0.0611	0.204818	160,930
26–30	13.15486	1,315,486	0.030378	0.101831	133,957
31–perp.	22.02436	2,202,436	0.015103	0.302061	665,270
			Capital value		2,000,000

Notes:
1. The deferred YP is the YP for 5 years at the equated yield times the PV in the previous column.
2. The deferred YP for the years over 30 is YP in perp. at the market capitalisation rate times the PV in the previous column.

An alternative would be to use the equation discussed earlier, which is the DCF model. This provides a solution for the YP by rearrangement of the terms (see Baum and Crosby, 1988, p.123):

$$\text{YP } n \text{ years} = \text{YP } t \text{ years @ } e \times \left[\frac{1 - \dfrac{(1+g)^n}{(1+e)^n}}{1 - \dfrac{(1+g)^t}{(1+e)^t}} \right]$$

Where the income is £1 per annum, the total term is n years, the rent review period is t years, the equated yield is e per cent and the growth rate is g per cent p.a.

By formula (spreadsheet layout)					
$\text{YP } n \text{ years} = \text{YP } t \text{ years @ } e \times \dfrac{1-(1+g)^n/(1+e)^n}{1-(1+g)^t/(1+e)^t}$					
Here n =	perpetuity and thus $(1 + g)^n/(1 + e)^n$ will tend to 0				
t =	5	years			
e =	15.00%				
g =	10.86%				
YP in perp. =		3.352155	×	1	
				0.167608	
	=	20			
Valuation:					
ERV		£100,000	p.a.		
YP whole term		<u>20</u>			
Capital value		£2,000,000	p.a.		

Equated rents

The valuation of equated rents or constant rents relates to the adjustment of comparables for non-regular rent review patterns. This is to take into account growth over a longer review pattern. K, the constant rent factor, is based on the formula:

$$K = \frac{A-B}{A-1} \times \frac{C-1}{C-D}$$

where *A* is the Amount of £1 @ *R*% (the equated yield) for *L* years (the actual abnormal review period);

B is the Amount of £1 @ *G*% (the growth rate for property of this type) for *L* years;

C is the Amount of £1 @ *R*% for *Z* years (normal rent review pattern); and

D is the Amount of £1 @ *G*% for *Z* years.

Example 10.5: Equated rents

Calculate the rent appropriate on rent review for a lease with 21-year rent reviews. The lessor's required return on capital is 15 per cent (equated yield) and the growth rate anticipated is 8 per cent. The estimated full rental value is £10,000 p.a. on a normal rent review pattern of 5 years.

$$K = \frac{\text{Amount of £1 @ 15\% for 21 years} - \text{Amount of £1 @ 8\% for 21 year}}{\text{Amount of £1 @ 15\% for 21 year} - 1}$$

$$= \frac{\text{Amount of £1 @ 15\% for 5 years} - 1}{\text{Amount of £1 @ 15\% for 5 years} - \text{Amount of £1 @ 8\% for 5 years}}$$

$$= \frac{18.8215 - 5.0338}{18.8215 - 1} \times \frac{2.0114 - 1}{2.0114 - 1.4693}$$

$$= 1.443$$

Thus the rent appropriate on review is:

K × Rent on normal review = 1.443 × £10,000 p.a. = £14,430 p.a.

SUMMARY OF CHAPTER

This chapter examined the yields and interest rates used in property valuation:

- It analysed the interest rate into its components.
- It has examined the equivalent and equated yields.
- It has investigated the implied rate of growth.

REFERENCES AND BIBLIOGRAPHY

Barkham, R. J., Ward, C. W. R. and Henry, O. T. (1995) 'The inflation-hedging characteristics of UK property', *Journal of Property Finance*, Vol. 7, No. 1, pp.62–76.

Baum, A. and Crosby, N. (1988) *Property Investment Appraisal*, Routledge, London.

Baum, A. and Crosby, N. (1995) *Property Investment Appraisal*, Routledge, London.

Brown, G. R. (1991) *Property Investment and the Capital Markets*, E. & F. N. Spon, London.

Crosby, N. (1992) *Reversionary Freeholds; UK Market Valuation Practice*, Research Paper, RICS, London.

Enever, N. and Isaac, D. (1995) *The Valuation of Property Investments*, Estates Gazette, London.

French, N. (1994) 'Editorial: Market Values & DCF', *Journal of Property Valuation and Investment*, Vol. 12, No. 1, pp.4–6.

Isaac, D. and Steley, T. (2000) *Property Valuation Techniques*, Macmillan (now Palgrave), London.

Matysiak, G., Hoesli, M., MacGregor, B. and Nanathakumaran, N. (1995) 'Long-term inflation-hedging characteristics of UK commercial property', *Journal of Property Finance*, Vol. 7, No. 1, pp.50–61.

Scarrett, D. (1991) *Property Valuation: The Five Methods*, E. & F. N. Spon, London.

Part 4:
Taxation and Statutory Valuations

11 Taxation

11.1 Introduction
11.2 The conventional approach to valuation
11.3 Net-of-tax valuations

AIMS AND OBJECTIVES

This chapter investigates net-of-tax calculations for freehold and lease-hold interests.

Key terms

Net and gross rates and 'grossing up' – Gross rates of income and yield are without tax deductions. Net are after tax. 'Grossing up' is the conversion of an income to a higher amount to allow for any tax deduction.

Example

If t = tax rate as a decimal:

$$\text{gross rate} \times (1-t) = \text{net rate}$$

and the grossing-up factor is:

$$\text{gross rate} = \text{net rate} \times \frac{1}{(1-t)}$$

so if t = 40 per cent = 0.04 and the net rate required for investment is 3 per cent, then the gross rate needed to provide this net rate is:

$$0.03 \times \frac{1}{0.06} = 0.05 = 5 \text{ per cent}$$

11.1 INTRODUCTION

Income is generally assessed for tax but the taxpayer is allowed various allowances and expenses against income, which reduces the tax payable.

Some investments, such as pensions, have a built-in tax relief. Other accounts may also have this advantage; the use of the ISA (a tax-free savings account) in the UK is an example of an investment where the income generated is considered gross. The net-of-tax return is important because this is the actual amount that the investor receives. For a given taxpayer, the combinations of gross return and tax payable are thus of interest.

Tax rates can change on a regular basis, thus the examples in this chapter look at idealised levels of taxation so that the calculation can be seen. The make-up of the taxation structure is complex. For instance there is, in the UK, likely to be a number of different incremental layers of payment as follows:

Tax rates and allowances in the UK – 2000/2001 Tax Year (year ends April 2001)

Income tax rates

Taxable income (after allowances)	Rate
0–£1,520	10%
£1,521–£28,400	22%
Over £28,400	40%

Personal tax allowances

Age	Rate
Up to 65	£4,385
65–74	£5,790
Over 74	£6,050

Notes: For those over 65, allowances are reduced if income is greater than £17,000. Married couple's allowance for those under 65 has been abolished.

Income from capital gains (Capital Gains Tax – CGT) is taxed with the income but there are allowances to be set against this. In addition to taxation on income and capital gains, there are other taxes which affect real estate. These are:

- rates or land/building tax, an annual tax for local services based on the assessed value of the property;
- VAT on building works, a value added tax on the cost of work, currently 17.5 per cent;
- a transfer tax on the purchase of houses called Stamp Duty.

Stamp duty was increased in the March 2000 budget. At the upper end, the rate varies as follows:

Purchase price	Rate of Stamp Duty
Under £60,000	Zero
£60,000 to under £250,000	1%
£250,000 to under £500,000	3%
Over £500,000	4%

The supposed effect of Stamp Duty is to dampen down boom conditions, in this case in the south-east of England; although some argue it has an opposite effect, reducing houses coming onto the market and thus pushing up prices. The Council of Mortgage Lenders in the UK has said that Stamp Duty distorts the market by concentrating house prices just below each tier (The Times, 2000).

So, in appraisal approaches the net-of-tax approach will be used to analyse the position of the individual, but gross rates need to be applied in the analysis of the market where buyers and sellers have a wide range of tax liabilities. This distinction between gross and net positions reflects the different approaches of valuation of exchange price in the market and the assessment of worth discussed previously in this book.

11.2   THE CONVENTIONAL APPROACH TO VALUATION

Using the conventional method of property valuation, the view is taken that the income from the investment will be treated for income or corporation tax purposes in the same way as any other source of income. For example, income from government stock is paid 'gross of tax' in the same way that rent is received by the investor. Incomes from investments, whether from stock, securities or different types of property, will be capitalised using the appropriate Year's Purchase for the rate of interest, reflecting the investment's security. By deducting tax at the standard rate from the incomes, the relative position of each investment will not be altered. For this reason, the conventional view is taken that tax need not be deducted as an outgoing from rent before capitalisation. Furthermore, as the tax position of investors can vary widely, nothing is gained when valuing for sale on the open market by deducting tax at an assumed rate.

Where interest is paid 'net of tax', the rate of interest must be 'grossed up' using the gross tax factor for the standard rate of tax. So when a Building Society quotes 'an investment rate of 12 per cent – gross equivalent of 16 per cent for tax payers at 25 per cent' this is arrived at by:

Investment rate	0.12
Gross tax factor @ 25%	1.333
Gross equivalent investment rate	0.16

Tax adjustment factors can be found in Parry's Tables.

If two investments are to be compared, one being quoted at a yield of 10 per cent gross of tax, the other at 8 per cent net of tax, it is necessary for the yields to be on the same basis. Assuming tax at a rate of 25 per cent:

Gross of tax yield	10.00%
Net tax factor @ 25%	0.75 (1 – tax rate)
Net of tax yield	7.5%

from which it can be seen the net yield quoted will give a higher return. Alternatively, the net-of-tax yield can be converted to gross by:

Net-of-tax yield	8.00%
Gross tax factor @ 25%	1.333 [1/(1 – tax rate)]
Gross of tax yield	10.66%

giving the same conclusion.

Leasehold interests

A fundamental factor considered by an investor is that the capital sum invested will be returned. In the case of freehold interests that last in perpetuity, that is, the income is infinite, the capital can be recovered at any time by selling the interest.

Where the income to be valued is terminable, that is, the income is finite, as is the case with leasehold interests, the conventional view is that an annual sinking fund should be established to replace the capital sum invested on termination of the interest. Such funds are in the form of an insurance policy maturing on expiry of the interest, the annual premium required being found from the income received; this is allowed for by capitalising the profit rent from the investment using the Dual Rate Year's Purchase factor.

It is imperative that an annual sinking fund investment should not fail, otherwise the capital will not be returned; such 'riskless' investments will have a low yield – typically about 5 per cent. However low the income generated by the investment, it is still a source of income subject to income tax that effectively reduces the yield from the policy, so the rate of interest must be 'netted down' to find the effective yield, as illustrated above. As a further example for a tax being paid at 40 per cent:

Policy rate of interest	5.00%
Net tax factor 40%	0.6
Effective yield	3.00%

Certain expenses may be incurred by an investor holding an interest in real property – for example, repairs and reinstatement insurance – which can be deducted from rental income before tax is assessed. An annual sinking fund premium is not such an allowable expense; in other words, the premium is subject to tax. However, if the premium is reduced by tax it will be insufficient to replace the capital sum, therefore it is necessary to 'gross up' the premium to an amount which after tax will leave the required premium.

Leasehold interests are conventionally valued using Dual Rate Year's Purchase Tables adjusted for tax:

Net rental value	£15,000	
Net rent paid	8,000	
Profit rent	7,000	
YP 4 yrs @ 9% & 3% (tax 40%)	2.048	
Estimated capital value		£14,336

That the required return was 9 per cent is further demonstrated by:

Profit rent		£7,000
Less Annual sinking fund:		
Capital to be replaced	£14,336	
ASF 4 yrs @ 3%	0.239	
Annual sinking fund	£3,426	
Gross tax factor @ 40%	1.667	
Total allowance for ASF		£5,711
Remaining income		£1,289

$$\text{Return on capital} = \frac{£1,289}{£14,336} \times 100 = 9 \text{ per cent}$$

The allowance of £5,711 for the annual sinking fund includes the tax to be paid. This can be seen by:

Sum allowed	£5,711
Less Income tax @ 40%	£2,284
Amount remaining for ASF premium	£3,427

It can be seen that when valuing leasehold interests using the conventional method, income tax has two effects:

1. the rate of interest earned on the ASF policy is reduced;
2. the annual premium for the policy is subject to tax.

As the term of years lengthens, the effect of taxation on the premium reduces because of the discounting factor. This can be seen by studying the YP factors:

YP 4 years @ 9% & 3%	3.039
YP 4 years @ 9% & 3% (tax 40%)	2.048
Effect of tax: 33% reduction	
YP 60 years @ 9% & 3%	10.402
YP 60 years @ 9% & 3% (tax 40%)	9.978
Effect of tax: 4% reduction	

Non-tax payers

Investors who are not subject to income tax, such as pension funds, are placed in a particularly advantageous position compared with tax-paying investors when purchasing leasehold interests, because obviously neither the sinking fund rate nor the annual premium is reduced. In the case of the above example, a non-tax payer valuation would be:

Profit rent	£7,000
YP 4yrs @ 9% & 5%	3.106
Value	£21,742

This is over 50 per cent more than the taxpayer's value.

11.3 NET-OF-TAX VALUATIONS

Freehold interests

As the conventional method generally disregards tax on income, analysis of comparable sales will normally be on the gross-of-tax basis.

Example 11.1: Freehold net-of-tax valuation

A freehold property recently let at the net rack rent of £8,000 has just been sold for £100,000. The yield will be:

$$\frac{8,000}{100,000} \times 100 = 8 \text{ per cent}$$

This yield represents what the investment market is prepared to accept for a gross-of-tax income of £8,000.

If a net-of-tax analysis is required, the tax paid by the investor must be deducted from the income. Assuming tax at 40 per cent, this will be:

Gross-of-tax income	£8,000
Less Tax @ 40%	£3,200
Net income	£4,800

$$\text{Yield} = \frac{£4,800}{100,000} \times 100 \text{ per cent} = 4.8 \text{ per cent}$$

On this basis, a valuation must be made by capitalising income using a net-of-tax yield:

Net-of-tax income	£4,800	
YP in perp. @ 4.8%	20.833	
Capital value		£100,000

A net-of-tax valuation will only be required for an investor whose tax liability is known. It will be seen that a net-of-tax analysis of an interest let at rack rent will produce the same rate as one on a gross basis. However, this is not the case where there is rent below rack rent for a term of years.

Example 11.2: Freehold net-of-tax valuation

Value a freehold income of £750 per annum to be received for 5 years and which then reverts to rack rent of £1,000. For simplicity, a yield of 10 per cent is used for the term and reversion.

Gross of tax

Rent		£750		
YP 5yrs @ 10%		3.791		
			£2,843	
Full rental value		£1,000		
YP perp. @ 10%	10.00			
PV £1 in 5yrs @ 10%	0.621			
		6.21		
			£6,210	
Capital value				£9,053

Net of tax

Rent	£750
Less Tax @ 40%	£300
Net-of-tax income	£450
YP 5yrs @ 6%	4.212
	£1,875

Full rental value		£1,000
Less Tax @ 40%		£400
Net-of-tax income		£600
YP perp. @ 6%	16.667	
PV £1 in 5yrs @ 6%	0.747	
	12.45	
		£7,470
Capital value		£9,345

Leasehold interests

The position regarding leasehold interests is the same as for freehold; namely the same result will be obtained for both the gross and the net-of-tax basis where there is a single profit rent. When valuing net of tax though, it is not necessary to use tax-adjusted Dual Rate YP tables, because the total income tax liability will be deducted before capitalisation.

Example 11.3: Leasehold net-of-tax valuations

Value on a gross and net basis a profit rent of £1000 to be received for 5 years, on which a yield of 10 per cent is required with a sinking fund of 3 per cent, the tax rate being 40 per cent.

Gross of tax

Profit rent	£1,000	
YP 5yrs @ 10% & 5% (tax 40%)	2.416	
Capital value		£2,416

Net of tax

Profit rent	£1,000	
Less Tax @ 40%	400	
Net-of-tax income	600	
YP 5yrs @ 6% & 3%	4.027	
Capital value		£2,416

There will be difference between gross and net-of-tax values where there is a term and reversion.

Example 11.4: Leasehold net-of-tax valuations

Value on a gross and net basis a profit rent of £750 to be received for 5 years followed by a profit rent of £1,000 for a further 5 years with the same conditions as before.

Gross of tax

Profit rent		£750	
YP 5yrs @ 10% & 3% (tax 40%)		2.416	
			£1,812
Profit rent		£1,000	
YP 5yrs @ 10% & 3% (tax 40%)	2.416		
PV £1 in 5yrs @ 10%	0.6209		
		1.5	
		£1,500	
Value			£3,312

Net of tax

Profit rent		£750	
Less Tax @ 40%		300	
Net-of-tax income		450	
YP 5yrs @ 6% & 3%		4.027	
			£1,812
Profit rent		£1,000	
Less Tax @ 40%		400	
Net-of-tax income		600	
YP 5yrs @ 6% & 3%	4.027		
PV £1 in 5yrs @ 6%	0.747		
		3.01	
		£1,806	
Capital value			£3,618

Generally, valuers hold the conventional view that because the property market consists of such a wide variety of investors, each having their own tax liability and strategies, there is little point in taking tax into consideration for open-market valuation purposes. With regard to analysis, however, taxation is of great importance.

SUMMARY OF CHAPTER

This chapter has introduced calculations made on a net-of-tax basis in respect of both freehold and leasehold properties.

REFERENCES AND BIBLIOGRAPHY

Isaac, D. and Steley, T. (1991) *Property Valuation Techniques*, Macmillan (now Palgrave), London.

The Times (2000) 'Gordon stamps all over Cabinet colleagues', *The Times*, 22 March, p.39.

12 Statutory Valuations

AIMS AND OBJECTIVES

This chapter introduces statutory valuations in the context of:

• business tenancies;
• landlord and tenant valuations;
• residential tenancies;
• rating.

Key terms

Business tenancies – based on the Landlord and Tenant Acts 1927 and 1954.
Annual equivalent rent – rent passing plus/minus any decapitalised capital payments/receipts.
Premium – a capital sum paid to reduce the annual rental.

12.1 BUSINESS TENANCIES

The legislation on business tenancies is found in the Landlord and Tenant Acts 1927 and 1954, the latter being amended by the Law of Property Act 1969. The statutory framework consists of the Landlord and Tenant Act 1927 part I and the Landlord and Tenant Act 1954 part II. These Acts deal with compensation for tenants, improvements and the procedures for ending the lease. Part II of the 1954 Act sets out a detailed code of the rights and duties at the termination of tenancies. The Law of Property Act 1969 has made amendments.

The key sections of the 1954 Act are:

s.23: this gives a broad interpretation of the definition of a business tenant as covered by the enactment.

s.43: this indicates the types of tenant covered by the Act and excludes tenants with interests of less than 6 months.

s.38: this provides the scenario whereby a joint application of the two parties to the lease contract can be made to the court to exclude the provisions of the Act.

Security of tenure

Section 24 of the Landlord and Tenant Act 1954 states that a business tenancy cannot come to an end unless terminated in accordance with the Act, that is by:

- notice to quit by the tenant, surrender or forfeiture;
- tenant's notice to terminate under s.27;
- landlord's notice to terminate under s.25;
- tenant's request for a new tenancy under s.26;
- landlord and tenant agreeing the grant of a new tenancy.

The landlord can oppose the grant of a new tenancy under section 30 of the Act on a number of grounds:

(a) tenant's breach of repairing obligations;
(b) tenant's persistent delay in the payment of rent;
(c) other serious breach of covenant;
(d) the provision of suitable alternative accommodation for the tenant;
(e) because the landlord wants to let the premises as a whole, which is more economical;
(f) because the landlord wants to demolish and reconstruct the premises;
(g) because the landlord wants to occupy the premises.

Section 24A of the Law of Property Act 1969 allows the landlord to apply to the court for an interim rent after notice has been given. This gives the landlord an opportunity to recover a rental close to the market rent during the period of negotiation.

New tenancy

Section 34 states that the rent on the new lease shall be the open-market rent, disregarding:

- any effect on the rental value of the tenant's previous occupation of the premises;
- any goodwill attaching to the premises;
- any effect on the rental of certain improvements;
- any value attributable to a liquor licence.

Improvements will be disregarded in the calculation of the new rent if they have been carried out other than as an obligation of the lease and if they have been carried out either during the currency of the existing lease or in the last 21 years before review. The legislation allows for compensation on quitting by the tenant and for improvements carried out by the tenant.

The lease will set out details of the arrangement of the rent reviews, particularly:

- the frequency of reviews;
- the basis of review (i.e. to open-market value, but this needs to take into account onerous clauses in the lease, tenant's improvements made to the premises and so on);
- the nature of the rent to be reviewed, whether it be upwards only, indexed, based on turnover and so on;
- the procedures for the review;
- procedures for arbitration in the event of the two parties disagreeing on the review.

12.2   LANDLORD AND TENANT VALUATIONS

Analysis of Landlord and Tenant valuations requires the conversion of any income and capital payments to an annual equivalent rent. This rent, also called the 'virtual rent', represents not only the rent paid but also the yearly equivalent cost of any capital sums paid, improvements carried out and the value of a surrendered lease. The virtual rent at the beginning of the lease should equal the ERV (estimated rental value). The annual equivalent is the yearly cost to a tenant of occupation which consists of:

1. interest on capital taken at the leasehold rate;
2. a sum to provide a sinking fund to recoup the expenditure over the unexpired portion of the lease. This sinking fund will be liable to tax, so it has to be grossed up to allow for any tax to be paid.

Example 12.1: The calculation of an annual equivalent

Estimate the annual equivalent rent of the following industrial unit: lease is for 25 years with a 5-year rent review on a full repairing and insuring basis

(FRI terms), the rent agreed is £5,000 p.a. and a premium of £200,000 has been paid. The freehold yield in the market is 6 per cent. The rent will be reviewed to the market level at the next review.

Approach

Assume leasehold yield to be 6 per cent plus 2 per cent risk premium, say 8 per cent. The rent will be reviewed in 5 years when the benefit of the premium will be lost. It is necessary to decapitalise the premium over the 5 year period to the review to find its income equivalent.

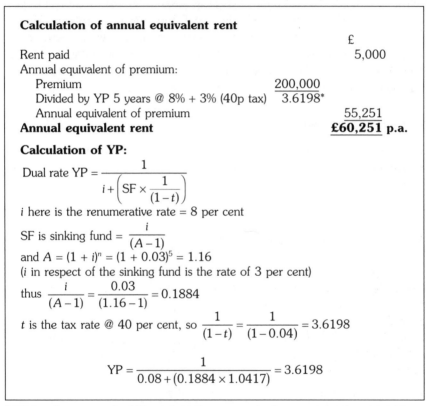

Calculation of annual equivalent rent

		£
Rent paid		5,000
Annual equivalent of premium:		
Premium	200,000	
Divided by YP 5 years @ 8% + 3% (40p tax)	3.6198*	
Annual equivalent of premium		55,251
Annual equivalent rent		**£60,251** p.a.

Calculation of YP:

$$\text{Dual rate YP} = \frac{1}{i + \left(SF \times \dfrac{1}{(1-t)} \right)}$$

i here is the renumerative rate = 8 per cent

SF is sinking fund = $\dfrac{i}{(A-1)}$

and $A = (1 + i)^n = (1 + 0.03)^5 = 1.16$

(i in respect of the sinking fund is the rate of 3 per cent)

thus $\dfrac{i}{(A-1)} = \dfrac{0.03}{(1.16-1)} = 0.1884$

t is the tax rate @ 40 per cent, so $\dfrac{1}{(1-t)} = \dfrac{1}{(1-0.04)} = 3.6198$

$$YP = \frac{1}{0.08 + (0.1884 \times 1.0417)} = 3.6198$$

* With reference to the YP used, in the approach above many valuers would use either a gross calculation (YP dual rate without tax) or use a single-rate calculation at the leasehold yield. We will see in later calculations that this means that the lessor's and lessee's view of the calculations are much closer and thus some of the negotiations suggested in landlord and tenant relationships become more feasible.

There are different types of application of valuation methods to landlord and tenant relationships, essentially these are about:

- payments of premium;
- surrender and renewal of leases;
- the treatment of improvements.

Premiums

A premium is a capital sum paid to reduce the level of rental to be paid; the rental is reduced by the annual equivalent of the premium. There are a number of advantages to the landlord and tenant of such an arrangement. For the landlord, the payment of such an amount by the tenant will reduce the rental usually below the market rental; thus the landlord's investment becomes very secure. The payment of such a premium would increase the cash flow position of the landlord and may have tax advantages. For the tenant, it may be advantageous to make this initial payment and reduce overheads.

Example 12.2: Premiums

If a shop lease is being sold on the following terms, what premium could be charged?

Data:

Full rental value	£10,000 p.a.
Rent passing	£2,000
Unexpired term on lease	5 years
Freehold yield at full rental value	6.00%
Leasehold yield, say plus 1%	7.00%

Lessee's proposed interest

Full rental value	£10,000 p.a.
Less Rent passing	£2,000 p.a.
Profit rent	£8,000 p.a.
YP 5yrs @ 7 + 3% (40p tax)	2.6047
Premium to be paid	£20,837

Lessor's proposed interest

Full rental value	£10,000

Less Annual equivalent of premium paid:

$$\frac{£20,837}{\text{YP 5yrs@6\%}} = \frac{£20,837}{4.2124} = £4,947$$

Rent required	£5,053

Calculation of yields

Leasehold yield $\quad i = 7.00\%$

$\quad\quad\quad$ SF rate $s = 3.00\%$

$\quad\quad\quad\quad\quad t = 0.4$

$\quad\quad\quad\quad\quad n = 5$

Dual rate YP = YP 5 yrs @ 8 + 3%(40p tax) = $\dfrac{1}{i + \left(SF \times \dfrac{1}{(1-t)} \right)}$ = **2.6047**

The spreadsheet equation is $1/(i + ((s/(((1 + s)\wedge n) - 1)) * (1/(1 - t6))))$

Freehold yield $i = 6.00\%$

$\quad\quad\quad\quad\quad n = 5$

YP = YP 5 yrs @ 6% = $\dfrac{1 - PV}{i}$ = **4.2124**

The spreadsheet equation is $(1 - (1/((1 + i)\wedge n)))/i$

This shows the premium to be paid as £20,837 from the lessee's point of view, but when we analyse from the lessor's point of view, the premium is insufficient and on the basis of this level of premium the lessor would look to increase the rental to £5,053 p.a. The discrepancy between the existing rent (£2,000) assumed by the lessee's calculation and the £5,053 revised rent in the lessor's view is a product of the difference of the yield rates used. For the lessor, this is a single rate of 6 per cent; for the lessee, is a dual rate adjusted for tax (7% + 3% (40p tax)). If we repeat the calculation using single rates for both parties:

Data:

Full rental value	£10,000 p.a.
Rent passing	£2,000
Unexpired term on lease	5 years
Freehold yield at full rental value	6.00%
Leasehold yield, say plus 1%	7.00%

Lessee's proposed interest

Full rental value	£10,000 p.a.
Less Rent passing	£2,000 p.a.
Profit rent	£8,000 p.a.
YP 5 yrs @ 7%	4.1002
Premium to be paid	£32,802

Continued

Lessor's proposed interest

Full rental value	£10,000
Less Annual equivalent of premium paid:	

$$\frac{£32,802}{\text{YP 5 yrs @6\%}} = \frac{£32,802}{4.2124} = £7,787$$

Rent required	£2,213

Calculation of yields

Freehold yield i = 6.00%   7.00%

$n = 5$ 5

$$YP = YP\ 5\,\text{yrs}\,@6\% = \frac{1-PV}{i} = \mathbf{4.2124}$$

$$YP = YP\ 5\,\text{yrs}\,@7\% = \frac{1-PV}{i} = \mathbf{4.1002}$$

Here the agreed new rent with the premium will be the compromise between the lessor's and lessee's view, say:

$$\frac{(£2,213 + £2,000)}{2} = \text{say, } £2,106$$

It might be that there would be a minor change in the rent here or in the premium to reflect the lessor's view. For the following calculation we will again use a single rate in the valuation of the lessee's interest so that the compromise position can be drawn out.

Surrender and renewal

The analysis of the premium can be further extended to surrender and renewal situations where a lessee might surrender a lease to renew and extend it to provide more security, especially if the tenant is thinking of carrying out works. A before-and-after scenario can be used. Imagine a situation where the existing lease has 4 years to run but the lessee wants a new lease for 5 years without review.

Example 12.3: Surrender and renewal

Lessee's present interest

Full rental value	£10,000 p.a.
Less Rent passing	£2,000 p.a.
Profit rent	£8,000 p.a.
YP 4 yrs @ 7%	3.3872
Value of interest	£27,098

We can compare this with the proposed interest from above: £32,802

Increase in value £5,704

Let present = proposed

£27,098 = £32,802 – premium (*P*)

P   =   £5,704

But this is the lessee's view. What difference will it make to the lessor?

Lessor's present interest

Term:

Rent reserved	£2,000 p.a.	
YP 4 yrs @ 5%	3.5460	
Value of term		£7,092
Reversion:		
Full rental value	£10,000 p.a.	
YP in perp. @ 6% defrd. 4 years	13.2016	
Value of reversion		£132,016
Total value		£139,108

Lessor's proposed interest: assumes rent remains same

Term:

Rent reserved	£2,000 p.a.	
YP 5 yrs @ 5%	4.3295	
Value of term		£8,659
Reversion:		
Full rental value	£10,000 p.a.	
YP in perp. @ 6% defrd. 5 years	12.4543	
Value of reversion		£124,543
Total value		£133,202

Let present = proposed

£139,108 = £133,202 + premium (*P*)

P   =   £5,906

Here the agreed premium will be the compromise between the lessor's and lessee's view, say:

$$\frac{£5,906 + £5,704}{2} = £5,805$$

Improvements

Improvements have to be disregarded under the 21-year rule of the Land-lord and Tenant Act 1927. Tenant's voluntary improvements will only be disregarded if they were completed during the current tenancy or completed less than 21 years before the rent review. If improvements are to be included in a calculation, then we can take the example used previously. Assume the lessee is thinking of spending £10,000 and this will increase the full rental value rental by 6 per cent. This calculation is done from the lessee's point of view only to show the example of the calculation:

Example 12.4: Improvements

Lessee's present interest

Full rental value	£10,000 p.a.
Less Rent passing	£2,000 p.a.
Profit rent	£8,000 p.a.
YP 4yrs @ 8 + 3% (40p tax)	2.0904
Value of interest	£16,723

Lessee's proposed interest

Full rental value	£10,000 p.a.
Add For improvements: £10,000 @ 6%	£600 p.a.
New full rental value	£10,600 p.a.
Rent to be reserved	x
Profit rent	£10,600 − x p.a.
YP 5yrs @ 8 + 3% (40p tax)	3.8846
Value of interest	£41,177 − 3.8846x
Less Cost of improvements	£10,000
Net value	£31,177 − 3.8846x

Let present = proposed

£16,723 = £31,177 − 3.8846x

x = £3,721

This shows the revised rent the lessee would want to pay.

Check:

Lessee's proposed interest

Value of lease	£16,723
Plus Improvements	£10,000
Capital value (assumes all improvement cost adds to value)	£26,723

The annual equivalent is:

$$\frac{£26,723}{\text{YP 7yrs @ 8 + 3\% (40p tax)}} = \frac{£26,723}{3.8846} = \underline{£6,879}$$

This represents the annual equivalent of the new position and can be checked against new full rental value *less* new revised rent to the lessor:

£10,600 *less*   £3,721 *equals*   £6,879 p.a. new profit rent

12.3   RESIDENTIAL TENANCIES

The majority of residential property is owner occupied but there is still a substantial private sector. The setting of legislation on the sector goes back to the Rent Acts of 1957 and 1965; this legislation had a *severe* effect on the market, creating rent control and security for tenants. The Acts created controlled and regulated tenancies paying controlled and fair rents. The Housing Acts of 1980 and 1988 provide a significant change to the legislation and gave rise to a number of tenancies, the four main areas of interest here are regulated tenancies, assured tenancies, assured shortholds and long leaseholds.

- *Regulated tenancies* are essentially those, as mentioned earlier, which were controlled or regulated prior to the 1980 and 1988 Acts.
- *Assured tenancies* under the 1988 Act are the basis for recent residential lettings. There is protection provided for the tenant but essentially the rents are at a market level.
- *Assured shortholds* are tenancies for a limited period with a minimum of six months.
- Long leasehold legislation has its origins in the 1967 Leasehold Reform Act although subsequent legislation has modified it. *Long leaseholders* under this and subsequent legislation have the rights, under certain conditions, to purchase the freehold of their property (termed *enfranchisement*) or else to extend the lease by 50 years. Rights to enfranchisement have been extended by the Leasehold Reform, Housing and Urban Development Act 1993.

12.4   RATING

Property is assessed for rates, which is a local property tax. General rate and water rates are calculated by applying the rate in the £ to the Rateable Value (RV) calculated. The assessment for rates is on a Gross Value (GV) basis or a Net Annual Value basis (NAV). The Gross Value basis is a calculation of the rent of the property let on an annual basis with the landlord being responsible for repairs and insurance. Net Annual Value (NAV) is the annual rent where the tenant is responsible for repairs and insurance. The principle of assessing the value is on the basis that:

- the property is vacant and to let;
- it is in its existing physical state (Latin expression: *rebus sic stantibus*);
- it takes into account actual rents passing on the property and the level of comparable rents;
- it is based on the 'tone of the list' which means that the rent value calculated must take into account the level of value in the rating list and reflect that general level of value.

Assessment methods include the rental method (based on comparable evidence), the contractor's method (where comparable market evidence is not available) and the profits method, used in the same way as the valuation method generally outlined in Chapter 5, where there is an element of monopoly in the property business.

SUMMARY OF CHAPTER

This chapter has introduced:

- The basis of business tenancies – security of tenure and the grant of new tenancies.
- Landlord and tenant valuations – premiums and surrender and renewals.
- Types of residential tenancies.
- A brief summary of rating.

Part 5:
The Development
Appraisal and Finance

13 The Development of the Residual Valuation

13.1 The detailed residual valuation
13.2 The calculation of the development profit
13.3 Sensitivity and risk

AIMS AND OBJECTIVES

This chapter sets out the detailed residual valuation and its various components. It explains how to calculate the development profit and allow for the variation of the inputs to the calculation where those inputs cannot be provided as spot figures. The elements are thus examined for their sensitivity.

13.1 THE DETAILED RESIDUAL VALUATION

Example 13.1: The detailed residual valuation

Key data

A site of 9,000 square metres is owned by the local authority.

A development brief prepared by the local authority has suggested that an appropriate development on the site would be a mixed commercial scheme incorporating:

Office space:	$5,280 \, m^2$ gross
Supermarket:	$3,000 \, m^2$ gross
Shop units:	20 at $125 \, m^2$ gross each

The local authority will agree to the demolition of buildings on site.
Two hundred car parking spaces will need to be provided, 50 being accommodated above the supermarket and the rest as surface car parking.

Building costs

Demolition and site preparation costs	£100,000
Offices	£500/m^2
Standard shop units	£300/m^2
Supermarket	£250/m^2
Surface car parking	£400 per space
Roof top car parking	£2,000 per space

The scheme will take 18 months to complete.

Rents and yield

Office rents are £70/m^2 on modern leases.
Shops/supermarkets let at £80/m^2 overall in the locality (based on net retail space).
Yield on the overall scheme is 7 per cent.

Making whatever assumptions are necessary, prepare an appraisal to determine whether the scheme is viable and determine the residual value of the land, or overall loss.

Calculation

Assumptions:

1. Gross area is quoted. To obtain a net area, deduct 20 per cent for offices, 10 per cent for shops and 10 per cent for supermarket to give the net retail space.
2. Yield – given at 7 per cent.
3. Sales costs, if investment is sold on at end of development period, should be deducted from the Gross Development Value. For simplicity, example assumes developer retains the site.
4. Deductions are:
   - total building costs (on gross areas);
   - fees on building costs (12.5 per cent);
   - finance on fees and building costs (building cost for half the building period, and fees at two-thirds building period as costs paid out gradually over contract);
   - finance rate is, say, base +9 per cent = 15 per cent (assume risky security);
   - contingency;
   - letting fees (15 per cent rental – assumes joint agents);
   - advertising;
   - profit as, say, 17 per cent GDV;
5. A void or letting period of 3 months is allowed for – interest is calculated on total sum for this period.

6. Amount of residual has to be discounted back to the beginning of the development period (18 months + 3 months void) *less* purchase costs.

Site appraisal

Gross Development Value
Supermarket – 3,000 m² gross
     less 10 per cent, say 2,700 m² net
     at £80 per m²   £216,000 p.a.
Shops – 20 at 125 m² gross
     less 10 per cent, say 110 m² net
     at £80 per m² = £8,800 × 20   £176,000 p.a.
Offices – 5,280 m² gross
     less 20 per cent, say 4,224 m² net
     at £70 per m²   £295,680 p.a.
     Total income   £687,680 p.a.
     Yield in perp. at 7 per cent   14.29 YP
     Gross Development Value   £9,826,947

Less Costs
Building costs
5,280 m² offices @ £500   £2,640,000
3,000 m² supermarket @ £250   750,000
125 m² shops × 20 × £300   750,000
Car park:
          150 at £400   60,000
          50 at £2,000   100,000
Demolition and site cost   100,000

Total building cost   £4,400,000
Fees at 12.5 per cent   550,000

Interest on half building cost for   495,000
     18 months at 15 per cent
Interest on two-thirds fees for   82,500
     18 months at 15 per cent
Total cost   £5,527,500
Interest on total for void period for   207,281
     3 months @ 15 per cent p.a.   £5,734,781
Add contingency at 3 per cent   172,043
                                                            £5,906,824

Letting fees at 15 per cent rent, say   95,000
Advertising 1 per cent GDV, say   90,000
Total Development Costs   £6,091,824
Plus developers profit at 17 per cent GDV   1,670,581
Costs plus profit   £7,762,405

Value of site in $1\frac{3}{4}$ year	£2,064,542	
× PV of £1 in $1\frac{3}{4}$ years at 15 per cent, say		0.783
Value of site now		£1,616,536
less Acquisition costs at 4 per cent	4,661	
Site value		£1,551,875
Site value that could be offered is, say	£1,550,000	

13.2 THE CALCULATION OF THE DEVELOPMENT PROFIT

The residual valuation shows how much to pay for the site. If the site value is already known, then this can be incorporated into the valuation to work out the developers profit. Using the figures from above, the capital profit on completion can be calculated, together with the annual profit.

(1) Capital profit on completion

Expected capital value		£9,826,947
Expected total costs:		
Building cost, fees and finance on total	£6,091,824	
Land cost	£1,550,000	
Finance on land cost @ 15 per cent over	£726,411*	
$2\frac{3}{4}$ years		£8,368,235
Residual profit		£1,458,712

* This is calculated by compound interest: $[£1,550,000 \times (1 + 0.15)^{2.75}] -$ £1,550,000. This is based on the Amount of £1 formula or compound interest.

Thus instead of the traditional residual calculation to find the site value, which is based on:

Gross Development Value *less* (Building Cost plus Profit) *equals* Residual Site Value or Land Cost

$$GDV - (BC + P) = LC$$

this is rearranged to:

Gross Development Value *less* Total Cost (which includes Land Cost) *equals* Profit

$$GDV - (BC + LC) = P$$

From the calculation:

Profit as a percentage of total cost $= \dfrac{£1,458,712}{£8,368,255} = 17.4$ per cent

$$\text{Profit as a percentage of capital value} = \frac{£1,265,000}{£9,826,947} = 14.8 \text{ per cent}$$

(2) Annual profit if scheme is retained as an investment

This assumes that the developer has funded the scheme from its own funds or else an investing institution has acted as developer. Say the developer requires a 7 per cent long-term yield.

Expected annual income	£687,680 p.a.
Expected total costs:	
Building cost, fees and finance on total	£6,091,824
Land cost	£1,550,050
Finance on land cost @15% over 2¾ years	£726,411
Total costs	£8,368,235

$$\text{Development yield} = \frac{£687,680}{£8,368,235} = 8.22 \text{ per cent}$$

Thus any return greater than 7 per cent could be the developers profit = 1.22 per cent.

So, in the residual valuation approach:

$$\text{Value} - \text{Cost} = \text{Profit on a capital basis}$$

and Development yield – Investment yield = Developer's profit on an annual basis

13.3 SENSITIVITY AND RISK

The traditional residual technique is not adequate to deal with a more complex development situation where expenditure and income are being made and received at different times over a long time scale. Greater accuracy can be achieved by using cash flow approaches – either:

- a cash flow method, using period-by-period cash flows on which interest can be charged;
- a discounted cash flow (DCF) method, as above except that the flows are discounted back to the present;
- a DCF approach, building inflation into costs and growth into rents.

Improved techniques do not solve all the difficulties of the calculation; the problem of a residual calculation is that changes in elements of the calculation can affect the final site value drastically. Sensitivity analysis looks at the various elements of the residual calculation in an attempt to distinguish those elements where change will most affect profitability. Attention can then be paid to such factors and steps taken to reduce the uncertainty.

Detailed application of sensitivity and risk are beyond this book, so here only an introduction is attempted into the variables involved. When we look at the residual valuation, we see that there are a number of variables in respect of the inputs to that valuation. These variables are subject to change and possible indications of these changes are indicated below.

1. *Land costs*
The land costs may be put in at the asking price but, in practice, if the appraisal does not produce a satisfactory developer's yield or profit, the scheme would have to be abandoned or some means found to reduce development costs. Because the land cost is a residual cost, it can therefore be negotiated.

2. *Ancillary costs of acquisition*
The ancillary costs of acquisition are made up of agent's fees, legal fees and Stamp Duty. Each of these is either the subject of a fixed scale or can be determined accurately prior to purchase. In any event, they comprise a small part of the total development cost, perhaps not more than 0.5 per cent.

3. *Pre-building contract period*
The period for which the land will be held, and therefore the period for which it has to be financed, is made up of three parts. Firstly, the period between the purchase of the land and the start of construction, which may be easy to assess if planning permission is already available. When no planning permission exists, the contract of purchase may be made subject to planning permission being granted, and the greater part of the land costs therefore will not be incurred until that time. The second period that has to be financed is the period of construction, and the third period is the period for letting and selling. If the property is speculative, you will need to assume that there is no rental income receivable before the completion of construction and that an additional period of perhaps three months needs to be allowed to secure a tenant and arrange for leases to be granted. Where the scheme is pre-let or pre-sold, this period may be eliminated.

4. *Short-term rate of interest*
Having established an estimated period for holding the land, it is necessary to apply an estimated rate of interest on short-term borrowing, to arrive at the cost of holding the land. The developer may have established sources

of funds or may have arranged specific short-term funds for the particular scheme. The estimated rate of interest will reflect current rates and possible future trends.

5. *Area of building*
If there is detailed planning consent, then the area of building is known from this consent, otherwise it will be based on discussion with the local authority and a consideration of what is physically possible. A common plot ratio for industrial buildings is 1:2, that is, one metre square of building space to each two metre square of land.

6. *Building costs*
The estimate of the cost of construction is a major element; it is affected by the level of inflation. The overall rate of increase in the building costs is made up of the increase in the cost of building materials and in the cost of labour. It is usual to allow foreseeable increases in wages and material costs, which can be reasonably estimated for perhaps six months or so ahead.

The Building Cost Information Service monitors the cost of projects and indicates possible changes. These could be built into prediction of future changes – see Box 13.1, which provides a summary of the fourth quarter of 1998.

7. *Professional fees*
In addition to the basic cost of construction, there are professional fees. Given the estimated building costs, they can be calculated fairly accurately as they are normally related to an established range of charges. The figure for fees may be made up as follows:

Architect	6%
Quantity surveyor	4%
Engineer	2%
Building Regulations' approvals, etc.	0.5%
Total	11.5%

8. *Building and letting period*
The length of the building period is important because it affects the cost of holding the land and the cost of short-term building finance. The normal convention is to assume that the building costs are spread evenly over the building period. The cost of construction has to be financed during the building period and for the period it takes to sell or let the completed project.

BOX 13.1: EXAMPLE FROM BCIS WEB PAGE (http://bcis.co.uk/review.html), updated 24 March 1999

A Review of the Construction Economy
Tender prices increase year on year

- Tender prices rose 5.0 per cent in the year to the fourth quarter of 1998.
- Tender prices fell by 0.7 per cent compared with the previous quarter.
- The *General Building Cost Index* rose 4.0 per cent in the year to the fourth quarter 1998.
- Materials costs rose 0.6 per cent in the past year, while nationally agreed wage rates rose 6.1 per cent.
- Materials prices are expected to rise below the predicted rate of inflation in the first year of the forecast, rising at around the rate of inflation over the following year.
- Wage awards are expected to be settled above the predicted level of inflation during the forecast period.
- Data on new orders for construction in the fourth quarter of 1998 was delayed. However, anecdotal evidence suggests that orders fell in the fourth quarter of 1998 compared with the previous quarter.
- Demand is expected to rise throughout the forecast period although the rate of increase for new construction work is likely to slow down considerably in 1999, rising a little in 2000. The commercial sector is anticipated to be the main contributor to growth, particularly through demand for entertainment projects, helped by Lottery and Millennium funding. PFI schemes should increasingly add to growth in the commercial sector with more schemes entering the construction phase.   **©BCIS Ltd** 1999

---

9. *Agent's fees*

The amount of the agent's fees is fairly easy to assess as it is normally charged in relation to some established scale of charges. Note, however, that fees are negotiable and that official scale fees have generally been abolished.

10. *Advertising costs*

The cost of advertising includes the cost of advertising the property and of preparing and distributing particulars. This item of cost is fairly easy to estimate and is normally a small percentage of the total development costs.

11. *Rental income*

The rental income is an estimate of the rent that will be achieved when the development is completed at the end of the development period. The convention is that appraisals are based on today's costs and rental values without allowing for inflation or real increases over the period of the development. Indeed, the conservative convention is to allow for some inflationary effect on building costs but to keep rental values to current levels. The rental income directly determines the developer's yield and indirectly the developer's profit which is related to capital value.

12. *Investor's yield*
Having established the estimate of rental income, the capital value of the completed project is arrived at by capitalising that income at the appropriate investor's yield, making allowance for the cost of disposal. The prime property market is compact and the flow of market intelligence comparatively efficient. Yields do, however, vary over time and, unless the investment is to be pre-sold, that is the terms for the eventual sale are agreed with an investor prior to the start of the development, the developer has to form a view of the yields that will prevail at the end of the project, perhaps some eighteen months on. Because of the difficulties of forecasting, it is not unusual to adopt current yields.

SUMMARY OF SECTION

- In this section we have looked at twelve elements which could affect the result of the residual calculation.

- The most important will be those that have the most effect on the result of the calculation.

- Our sensitivity analysis will inform us which has the most effect. Sensitivity is explained later.

The most important elements in the calculation will depend on the project, but are likely to be (in order):

1. investor's yield (this will determine the gross development value);
2. rent (this will determine the gross development value);
3. building cost;
4. finance charges (determined by interest rate and development period).

Sensitivity testing

Small changes in individual inputs lead to larger changes in the residual answer; sensitivity testing is a way of examining the effects. A simple example is set out below which shows the effect of changes on two different development appraisals, one with a low land value and the other with a high land value.

	Development on prime site (land cost high in proportion to other costs)	Development on cheap site (land cost low in proportion to other costs)
GDV	£1,000,000	£1,000,000
Total costs (inc. finance)	£700,000	£900,000
Land value	£300,000	£100,000

Assume three scenarios for the above appraisals:

(i) value and cost increase by the same percentage;
(ii) value increases more than cost;
(iii) cost increases more than value

(i) *Value and cost increase in the same proportion. In this case, land value will increase in the same proportion.*
(ii) *Value increases by 30 per cent, cost by 10 per cent.*

	Prime development site	Cheap site
GDV	£1,300,000	£1,300,000
Total costs	£770,000	990,000
Land value	£530,000	310,000
Percentage change	+77%	+210%

Thus, if value increases by more than cost, it affects land value more if the land value is small in proportion to the total value of the development.
(iii) *Value increases by 10 per cent, cost by 20 per cent.*

	Prime development site	Cheap site
GDV	£1,100,000	£1,100,000
Total costs	£840,000	£1,080,000
Land value	£260,000	£20,000
Percentage change	−13%	−80%

The effect on the land value where the land value is a small proportion of total value is again more dramatic, illustrating the concept of gearing.

SUMMARY OF CHAPTER

- This chapter has provided a detailed residual valuation.
- It has examined the developer's profit calculation in this context.
- It has begun to look at applying the concepts of sensitivity and risk in the calculations used in development valuation.

REFERENCES AND BIBLIOGRAPHY

BCIS (1999a) *Quarterly Review of Building Prices*, BCIS, issue no. 73, March.

BCIS (1999b) *Review of the Construction Economy*, BCIS, Web page (http://bcis.co.uk/review.html), 24 March.

Britton, W., Davies, K. and Johnson, T. (1989) *Modern Methods of Valuation*, Estates Gazette, London.

Butler, D. and Richmond, D. (1989) *Advanced Valuation*, Macmillan (now Palgrave), London.

Cadman, D. and Austin-Crowe, L. (1991) *Property Development*, E. & F. N. Spon, London.

Davidson, A. W. (1989) *Parry's Valuation and Investment Tables*, Estates Gazette. London.

Isaac, D. (1996) *Property Development Appraisal and Finance*, Macmillan (now Palgrave), London.

Isaac, D. and Steley, T. (2000) *Property Valuation Techniques*, Macmillan (now Palgrave), London.

Morley, S. (1988) 'The residual method of valuation', in C. Darlow (ed.), *Valuation and Development Appraisal*, Estates Gazette, London.

Ratcliffe, J. and Rapley, N. (1986) 'Development properties', in W. H. Rees (ed.), *Principles into Practice*, Estates Gazette, London.

Royal Institution of Chartered Surveyors (1995) *Valuation of Development Land*, Draft consultation paper, January, RICS, London.

Seeley, I. H. (1995) *Building Economics*, Macmillan (now Palgrave), London.

14 Property Finance

14.1 Introduction
14.2 Categories of finance
14.3 Sources of finance
14.4 Lending criteria

AIMS AND OBJECTIVES

This chapter aims to consider the structure of property finance, the categories and sources of finance and the lending criteria on which finance is granted.

14.1 INTRODUCTION

The sorts of questions which may be key in our understanding of what finance is all about in a generalised corporate context are:

- What long-term investment strategy should a company take on?
- How can cash be raised for the required investments?
- How much short-term cash flow does a company need to pay its bills?

These are strategic decisions that will determine the strategy for generating cash and at the same time ensure that the company is liquid.

One way that companies raise cash to finance their investment activities is by selling or issuing securities. These securities are also called financial instruments or claims, as they are claims on the cash and assets of the company. Such securities may be roughly classified as equity or debt, and are loosely called respectively stock or bonds in the US and shares and loan stock in the UK. The differences in terminology do make this a problem when dealing with finance literature from the US. Sometimes the basic concepts behind a security or its operation may differ, as in the operation of financial options.

The difference between equity and debt is a basic distinction of the modern theory of finance, and this book uses the distinction to classify the

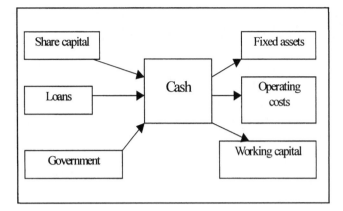

Figure 14.1　*The importance of cash*

instruments available. To summarise, all the securities of a firm are claims that depend on or are contingent on the value of the firm. Maximising shareholder's wealth is the primary goal of the company and thus financial decisions are made to increase value for shareholders. A company raises cash by issuing securities to the financial markets. There are two basic types of financial markets: the money markets and the capital markets. Money markets deal with debt securities that pay off in the short term, usually less than one year. Capital markets are the markets for long-term debt and equity shares.

The cash flow approach to the firm is shown in Figure 14.1.

The balance sheet model of the firm

The concept of the finance function as a corporate activity can be seen easily in the use of a balance sheet model of the firm (Ross *et al.*, 1993). The balance sheet is a yearly snapshot of the assets and liabilities of the firm. These approaches, besides looking at the application of company funds for the purchase of assets, also differentiate between the sources of the funds, in particular the difference between long-term debt and shareholders' equity in the firm (see Figure 14.2). An understanding of the difference between equity and debt is fundamental to an understanding of how finance works. The structure of finance can analysed in two different ways:

- Debt *v.* equity;
- Project *v.* corporate funding.

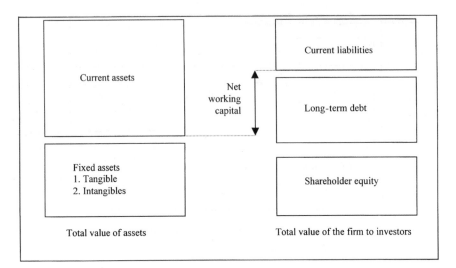

Figure 14.2 *The balance sheet model of the firm [Ross et al., 1993]*

In the past, most interest in property finance concentrated on project finance but with the size of schemes increasing and innovatory techniques of funding derived from the US and other economic sectors, there is now more interest in corporate finance. Generally, firms offer two basic types of securities to investors: debt securities are contractual obligations to repay corporate borrowing; equity securities are shares of common stock and preferred stock that represent non-contractual claims on the residual cash flow of the firm. Issues of debt and equity that are publicly sold by the firm are then traded on the financial markets. These distinctions between equity and debt and between project and corporate finance are clarified in the following paragraphs.

Debt v. equity

Equity is money and resources provided by the developer, partners, investors and funds who participate in the risk and profit of the scheme. Debt finance basically consists of loans raised from banks and other sources against the project (project specific) and non-project specific loans raised in the market. This is not always a useful distinction as corporate funding, the raising of finance against the assets of a company, can be based on equity as well as debt.

Project v. corporate finance

Project finance is finance provided where the principal or only security for the finance is the property itself, although supporting guarantees and additional collateral may also be requested. Corporate finance is finance raised on the back of the corporate entity rather than the project. Traditionally, property and other companies provided funds for new projects from retained earnings, the issue of new share and borrowings. In the post-war era, fixed interest mortgages and debentures were also used. Nowadays, there may be a complex corporate package of different types of funds.

Using the parameters above, the funding matrix can distinguish among the financing methods available and this is shown in Table 14.1.

Capital structure

Financing arrangements determine how the value of a company is sliced up. The persons or institutions that buy debt from the firm are creditors. The holders of the equity shares are shareholders. The size of the company's balance sheet will determine how well the company has made its investment decisions. The size of the firm is its value in the financial markets:

$$V = D + E$$

Value of company = Value of debt + Value of equity

[Ross *et al.*, 1993]

Corporate securities issued are a contingent claim on the value of the company. The shareholders' claim on the value of the company is a residual after payment to the debtholder; they get nothing if the value of the company is equal to or less than the amount promised to the debt holders.

Table 14.1   Funding matrix

	Corporate funding	**Project finance**
Equity finance	Share issues	Partnership funds Single asset unitisation
Debt finance	Loan stock Fixed interest debentures	Bank overdrafts Short-term funds for development

Capital structure and gearing

The basic points relating to capital structure and gearing are:

- money lent to the business by third parties is debt finance or loan capital;
- most companies borrow money on a long-term basis by issuing stocks or debentures;
- the supplier of the loan will specify the amount of loan, rate of interest, date of payment and method of repayment;
- the finance manager of a firm will monitor the long-term financial structure of the firm by examining the relationship between loan capital (where interest and loan repayments are contractually obligatory) and ordinary share capital (where dividend payment is at the discretion of the directors);
- this relationship between debt and equity is called gearing (known in the US as leverage) – strictly, gearing is the proportion of debt capital to total capital in the firm;
- the capital structure of a property company is a key factor in how a company is viewed in terms of its attractiveness for an investor or lender;
- the property sector was characterised by a high level of gearing because of the availability of fixed interest finance during the first post-war boom from 1954 to 1964, and this has occurred in subsequent boom periods;
- high gearing is of benefit when property values are rising ahead of interest charges, but can be dangerous if the real rate of interest is rising at a greater rate than property values.

An example of financial gearing is shown in Box 14.1.

Financial markets

The financial markets are composed of the money markets and the capital markets. Money markets are the markets for debt securities that pay off in the short term (usually less than 1 year). Capital markets are the markets for long-term debt and equity shares. Primary markets are used when governments or companies initially sell securities. Companies offer their shares through public placings or public offerings, and this is discussed in greater detail later in this chapter. Secondary markets come into operation for the resale of securities. Debt and equity are traded in the security markets, and there is a distinction between auction markets and dealer markets: equity securities tend to be sold in auction markets (like the stock exchange); debt securities are sold in dealer markets. Auction markets differ from dealer markets in two ways:

BOX 14.1: GEARING

GEARING
Example of the effect of gearing in house purchase

House is purchased for £100,000
The growth rate in house prices is 20 per cent
70 per cent is borrowed on mortgage
The interest rate on the mortgage is 10 per cent p.a.
The house is sold after 1 year

1. What is the equity return?
2. What is the return if you borrow 50 per cent?

1. Sale price	£120,000
Less Mortgage	£70,000
Plus Interest	£7,000
Balance	£77,000
Profit	£43,000

$$\text{Return on capital} = \frac{£43,000}{£30,000} \times 100 \text{ per cent} = 143 \text{ per cent}$$

$$= 43 \text{ per cent profit}$$

2. Sale price	£120,000
Less Mortgage	£50,000
Plus Interest	£5,000
Balance	£55,000
Profit	£65,000

$$\text{Return on capital} = \frac{£65,000}{£50,000} \times 100 \text{ per cent} = 130 \text{ per cent}$$

$$= 30 \text{ per cent profit}$$

1. Trading in an auction exchange takes place at a single site on the floor of the exchange or with a centralised screen system. In October 1986, the stock exchange changed its system of trading, post 'Big Bang' (the deregulation of the Stock Exchange), from trading on the floor of the exchange to an electronic marketplace. The Stock Exchange Automated Quotation System (SEAQ) moved the system of trading into dealing rooms equipped with computer screens.

2. The transaction prices of shares traded on the auction exchange are communicated almost immediately to the public by means of computers and other devices, but this is not so in dealer markets (Ross *et al.*, 1993).

Direct investment *versus* property vehicles

The concept of project *versus* corporate finance can be looked at from a different perspective, that of direct investment in property as against investment through a property vehicle. Venmore-Rowland (1991) has considered the advantages and disadvantages of investment by these two approaches, and these are shown in Box 14.2.

There are two factors that are working in opposite directions in the investment strategy; these are correlation to other investments and liquidity. Correlation is important to obtain a diversified portfolio of investment and therefore to spread risks. Direct property has a relatively low correlation to equities but is more illiquid. Property vehicles are liquid but are more highly correlated to equities (Venmore-Rowland, 1991).

BOX 14.2: DIRECT PROPERTY AND PROPERTY VEHICLES

DIRECT PROPERTY

Advantages	**Disadvantages**
Low risk relative to equities	Illiquid
Diversification benefits	Management intensive
Hedge against inflation	Minimum portfolio size required
Good for matching inflation-prone long-term liabilities	

PROPERTY VEHICLES

Advantages	**Disadvantages**
Liquidity	Loss of control
Divisibility	Tax slippage
Management expertise	Short term, relatively poor performance
Specialisation of vehicle	High correlation to stock market
Gearing	
Can shift weight/exposure	
Income benefits from the discount to net asset value	

14.2   CATEGORIES OF FINANCE

This section is based on a suggested classification by Brett (1990) and is summarised in Box 14.3.

Debt or equity

The distinction between debt and equity depends on whether the money is borrowed (debt), and here the lender has no direct involvement in the project, or whether the money has been invested on the basis of sharing both the risk and the returns of the project (equity). Borrowed money needs to be repaid, and interest will be paid on the outstanding amount until the debt is repaid. The equity return for the person who puts up the money is determined by the success of the enterprise. The person shares the profits and if there are none, then there is no return.

BOX 14.3: SUMMARY OF CATEGORIES OF FINANCE

Categories of finance
Debt or equity
Project finance or corporate finance
Loan or traded security
Secured or unsecured
Fixed rate or variable rate
Long term or short term
Recourse, non-recourse, limited recourse

Main criteria

- Debt or equity
- Project or corporate finance

Finance matrix

	Debt	Equity
Project finance		
Corporate finance		

The most obvious form of equity is ordinary share capital. Equity shares can also exist in development situations where a financier is entitled to a share in profits of the scheme. There are also deferred forms of equity such as convertible loans, which start as debt instruments paying a fixed rate of interest but later the loans may be converted into equity shares.

Project finance or corporate finance

Project finance is the money borrowed for a project, usually a development project. The loan is based on the project itself and this becomes the main security. A larger company may be able to borrow on the strength of the assets of the company itself rather than its individual projects; this is asset based or corporate finance. Interest will generally be lower for corporate loans than for project loans because there will be more collateral available for security rather than relying on the risk of a single project. Many companies are undertaking developments of such a size that they dwarf the company's own resources and the developer may then be concerned that, if anything went wrong with the project, the lenders may have recourse to other assets of the company, which may undermine the company's financial position. In this case, each development may need to be financed separately on a project basis and developers may try to make the project 'off-balance sheet' if possible.

Loan or traded security

Borrowed money may simply be a simple loan or a bond in the form of an instrument (a negotiable piece of paper) which is transferable. This is a form of IOU note and is called a security rather than a straightforward loan, and this can be sold on to other investors. The purchasers receive interest each year and also have the right for the original cost to be repaid at the end of the agreed duration of the security. If the purchasers do not wish to wait for this repayment date they can sell the rights to other investors, who then become entitled to receive the interest and the eventual repayment monies. Securities of this kind are bought and sold on the stock market.

Secured and unsecured

Lenders will normally require security for the money they provide; they want collateral (security) for the loans and thus will charge assets to cover the loan, either the specific assets of a business related to the project or the assets of a business as a whole. If the borrower fails to pay the interest or capital repayments as required, then the lender can put a receiver into the company, and the receiver will repay the loans from the proceeds of the sale of the company's assets or other available revenues. A secured loan is safer than an unsecured loan but well-established companies may be able to raise unsecured loans because the safeguard for the lender is the company's established profit record out of which the interest can be paid. Most borrowings in the euromarkets are unsecured, as are borrowings in the commercial paper market. The company's name and standing are the main guarantees.

Fixed rate or variable rate (floating rate) interest

Sometimes the rate of interest is agreed at the outset of the loan and remains unchanged over the life of the loan. With other loans, the interest rate will change according to movements in money market rates or other rates agreed. For large-scale floating rate borrowings, the most common yardstick of interest rates is the London Inter Bank Offered Rate or LIBOR. This is the rate of interest at which the banks themselves are prepared to lend to each other. It is agreed at the outset that the company will pay a margin over the LIBOR rate, say 2.5 percentage points (or 250 basis points, which is the same thing, as a basis point is 0.01 per cent) over LIBOR. You can choose a LIBOR floating rate and then fix it. Short-term borrowings are most likely to be at the floating rate of interest. Long-term borrowings, such as mortgage debentures, are more likely to be at a fixed rate. The borrower can buy a cap for floating rate borrowing. This is a form of insurance policy that means whatever happens to interest rates in general, a maximum limit is set to the interest rate that a borrower will have to pay.

Long term or short term

Loans are usually over a period between 1 and 30 years. This range contains short- and long-term loans but the boundaries of the two and the intermediate area between are not clearly defined. Many people consider 1–2 years to be short term, equivalent to the development period for most projects, 2–7 years as medium term and more than 7 years as long term. Overdrafts are technically payable on demand and thus are short-term borrowing, but many companies have an overdraft outstanding almost indefinitely. With a multi-option facility (MOF), a company might technically be borrowing for 3 months at a time. At the end of three months it repays the original loans and takes out new ones for another 3 months. If the facility runs for 5 years, effectively it has the use of 5-year money by 'rolling over' (Brett, 1990).

Recourse, non-recourse or limited recourse loans

If the loan for a particular project or for a particular subsidiary company is guaranteed by the parent, the lender has recourse to the parent, so can claim on the assets of the parent. If the only security for the lender is the project itself, as in a pure form of project-based finance, and the parent company has given no guarantees, the loan is non-recourse. A non-recourse loan is very unlikely to be granted in practice, because banks would generally require the loans to be limited recourse. The parent may have guaranteed interest payments but is under no obligation to repay the loan itself in these circumstances. A limited recourse loan would still depend on the reputation of the borrower and the track record of the company as well as the quality of the project itself.

Domestic or euromarket loans

Loans can be raised in the UK or in the euromarkets. Euromarket loans can be in sterling abroad (eurosterling) or other currencies (eurodollar). A company may well raise monies in the euromarkets in different currencies and then swap to sterling if sterling is not popular at the time of raising the funds. The terms and conditions of operation in the European market can be different; for instance euro-loans are often unsecured.

14.3 SOURCES OF FINANCE

The main lenders in the market are:

1. high street/clearing banks;
2. foreign banks;
3. building societies;
4. merchant banks;
5. insurance companies; and
6. finance houses.

As an example, data on the sources of money flowing into property during the boom-slump period of the property cycle in the 1980s and early 1990s are shown in Table 14.2.

Table 14.2 New money into property (CSO, 1994)

	Pension funds	Insurance companies	Banks	Property companies	Overseas	Total
			£ million			
1980	908	855	72	147	100	2,082
1981	843	1,073	469	97	70	2,552
1982	797	1,059	822	263	120	3,061
1983	680	845	934	83	85	2,627
1984	997	744	963	237	65	3,006
1985	590	815	1,691	344	90	3,530
1986	434	821	2,224	737	150	4,306
1987	240	755	3,998	2,300	290	7,583
1988	312	1,102	7,954	761	1,897	12,026
1989	92	1,510	10,622	1,647	3,267	17,138
1990	−491	1,080	7,066	164	3,269	11,088
1991	467	1,483	678	1,270	1,551	5,449
1992	349	600	−1,708	334	1,232	807
1993[a]	299	232	−3,248	1,957	1,514	754
1994[b]	−282	1,868	−1,546	1,280	—	1,320

[a] External figures to September.
[b] Not including external: 1994 figures are for first two quarters only; to September for property companies.

High street/clearing banks

The big four clearing banks are LloydsTSB, Barclays, National Westminster (owned by the Royal Bank of Scotland) and Midland (owned by HSBC). These are probably the first port of call for people looking for loans, especially if they have established relationships as account holders. However, these banks are conservative and may view new transactions related to property in a less than enthusiastic way. Smaller banks may be more useful potential funders. The smaller banks are likely to have less of a bad-debt problem and may want to increase market share. The larger banks have been burdened by over-exposure to the property sector and the emphasis over a period has been on debt repayment rather than new lending. British Clearing Banks' exposure to the property sector at the critical period to the end of the 1980s is shown in Figure 14.3.

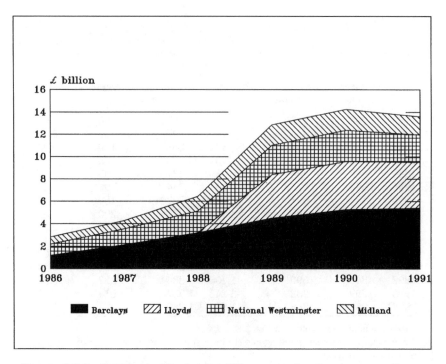

Figure 14.3 *British clearing banks' UK property lending (note: no figures for Lloyds 1986–88) [IBCA/Scott, 1992, p.348]*

Foreign banks

The foreign banks tend to be more aggressive sources of property finance, or were in the early 1990s, but by 1993 they were showing less interest. They are useful sources of funding, particularly for quality and corporate transactions. The collapse of certain foreign banks made borrowers wary of dealing with foreign banks. The collapse of a bank half-way through a development may mean that it could take years to unwind the legal problems and thus would put the borrower's own financial position at risk.

Building societies

The building societies fared badly in the 1990–95 slump in the property market. In the late 1980s, their inexperience and desire for market share in commercial property lending led to substantial bad debt. They are now putting their respective houses in order with rationalisation and more qualified staff, and are likely to be an important source of commercial finance in the future.

Merchant banks

Merchant banks rarely lend their own money but act as advisers and especially concentrate on large corporate transactions. They are unlikely to be interested in ordinary debt transactions because there would be little opportunity to use their expertise and add value to such a transaction.

Insurance companies

The insurance companies are limited providers of funds. They do, however, offer the attraction of long-term, fixed rate funds priced over gilts that can be useful in certain transactions.

Finance houses

In essence, the finance houses have been the principal providers of funding to the secondary leisure and retailing markets, providing finance for the purchase of freehold shops, pubs, restaurants and hotels. Their small trader exposure has made them particularly vulnerable to the latest recession, which has resulted in most of them leaving the market.

The growth of institutional investment

Institutions investing in the capital market in the UK are suppliers of finance to companies. These institutional investors include insurance companies, pension funds, investment trusts and unit trusts. Since the Second World War, institutional investors have increased their share of finance to firms at the expense of private individual investors. At the turn of the century, individual investors were very important on the stock markets but since that time progressive taxation and increased egalitarianism have reduced the differences in income between the very rich and poor, and thus enabled the poorer sections of society to accumulate some form of insurance within the insurance companies' funds. Thus, with the decline of the large private investors, there has been an increase in the amount of investment from the less affluent sections of society. These have tended to invest their money in building societies, unit trusts, insurance companies and saving banks, and these institutions have in turn provided their funds to the stock markets.

Government finance

Government finance is available to developers to assist in developing sites in certain locations under certain criteria. The loans available include money for City Grants and allowances in Enterprise Zones and urban development corporation areas. Assistance is also provided through the Simplified Planning Zones. The City Grant came into operation on the 3 May 1988. This replaced the Urban Development Grant and the Urban Regeneration Grant. To quality for a City Grant, it is necessary for the developer to prove that the development project cannot proceed without such a grant and that the project will benefit a run-down city area. In March 1993 it was announced that the Urban Programme of government funding would be phased out; this formed a major part of the government's urban renewal expenditure along with City Grants, Derelict Land Grants, Urban Development Corporations, City Action Teams and City Challenge. Under the Leasehold Reform, Housing and Urban Development Act 1993, the government established English Partnerships (EPs) to take over policy decision-making, to complement regional policy, to administer the English Industrials Estates Corporation, to buy and develop inner city sites, to assume the responsibility of the Urban Programme to award City Grants and Derelict Land Grants, and to administer City Challenge. A Single Regeneration Budget was created in 1994 to include expenditure on Urban Development Corporations, English Partnerships activities, Housing Action Trusts and other programmes.

Money for property development is also available from the European Community, especially funds for run-down or economically depressed locations.

14.4 LENDING CRITERIA

The cost and availability of lending are a function of the value of any particular project and the amount of cost to be financed. The nature of the development is important – the design, mix, location and likely demand. The letting conditions are important, as are whether or not the investment is pre-let or speculative. The quality of the tenant, who will be providing the cash flow to the investment, will also be important. Other important criteria are the track record of the developer and the strength of security. Finally, the duration of the loan will be important, as well as the details of repayment, for instance, the anticipated regularity of repayments, and the size/amount of repayments prior to redemption.

Most lenders look for the same aspects of a lending proposal, which in simplified terms are the four 'Cs':

- Character;
- Cashstake;
- Capability;
- Collateral.

Character

This relates to the trading history or development experience of a borrower. In respect of a property developer or an investment company, the lender will want to know whether the borrower has the experience to complete the development, manage the investment or run the business, if applicable. The lender will also be interested in whether the client is respectable and trustworthy. The lender may also cynically wonder why the borrower's own high street bank will not lend the money.

Cashstake

This relates to how much equity (the borrower's own money) is going into the transaction. In addition, the bank will want to know where the equity has come from:

1. Is it lent by someone else?
2. Is it from other profitable activities?
3. Is it simply a surplus that has arisen on the revaluation of property?
4. Is it already pledged as security?
5. Is it legally acquired money – not laundered money?

Capability

Does the borrower have the capability to service the loan, that is to pay the interest when it arises and the capital as and when repayment is required? Does the borrower have accounts or a business plan to show his/her present financial position and any estimate of future cash flow?

Collateral

The lender will want to know what security will be offered for the loan, its value and its saleability. The lender will want to know who valued the security and on what basis. The lender will need to assess the extent of the loan that would be exposed to the value of that security. Finally, will personal guarantees be given by the borrower?

Information required to approach a lender

When you approach a lender to obtain funds, you should ensure that you are clear on what finance you require and also ensure that you provide sufficient background information as follows:

• *Amount and purpose*
Specify the amount you wish to borrow and its purpose, e.g. acquisition of property, goodwill, fixtures and fittings etc.

• *Borrower's details*
The borrowing company's name trading and registered address accountant, banker and solicitor, together with the company's authorised and paid-up share capital, and a breakdown of shareholders and their respective holdings are all required.

• *Directors'/shareholders' details*
CVs of the directors/shareholders and the background or history of any parent company are needed. Where the borrower is a sole trader partnership, the lenders will require CVs together with personal asset and liability statements and copies of partnership agreements, where relevant.

• *Accounts*
Audited accounts for the borrower over the previous three years are essential.

• *Bank borrowing*
A breakdown of all current borrowings, i.e. mortgages and overdrafts, is needed. Also details of hire purchase agreements, leasing, identification of each lender and how each facility is secured.

• *Development activity*
Where the borrower is building or extending premises, the lenders need full details of the development, to include a description, breakdown of costs, warranties, copies of planning permission, details of contractor and building contract, and a full set of drawings.

• *Financial status*
The amount and availability of borrower's equity together with cash flow forecasts to support borrowing request are needed.

• *Background*
Other relevant information, as necessary, should be requested.

Recent research has shown that the presentation of funding proposals is very important in obtaining finance (Isaac and O'Grady, 1993).

Exercise question

Distinguish between debt and equity finance in the application of these types of finance to a property development project.

Outline answer

Equity and debt finance should be defined in the context of the developer using two types of monies. Firstly, those which are borrowed in the short term for the development period, and which need to be repaid with interest (i.e. debt); and secondly, money loaned in the long term which is subject to the risk of any enterprise but which shares in the profitability (i.e. equity). The distinction between the two is becoming blurred and this should be discussed. The application of these types of finance basically relates to the application of loans to a development project or the use of a company's own resources. You need to reflect on how to raise equity finance. At present, finance climate project loans may be becoming more difficult and perhaps more expensive to raise for risky developments.

SUMMARY OF CHAPTER

This chapter has introduced the basic principles of property finance including:

• The structure of finance.
• Categories of finance.
• Sources of finance.
• Lending criteria.

REFERENCES AND BIBLIOGRAPHY

Bank of England (1994a) *Quarterly Bulletin*, Vol. 34, No. 3, August.

Bank of England (1994b) *Quarterly Bulletin*, Vol. 34, No. 4, November.

Brett, M. (1983) 'Indirect investment in property', in C. Darlow (ed.), *Valuation and Investment Appraisal*, Estates Gazette, London.

Brett, M. (1990) *Property and Money*, Estates Gazette, London.

Cadman, D. and Austin-Crowe, L. (1991) *Property Development*, E. & F. N. Spon, London.

Central Statistical Office (CSO) (1994) *Financial Statistics*, November, CSO.

Chesterton Financial (1994) *Property Lending Survey*, February, Chesterton Financial, London.

Darlow, C. (1988a) 'The supply and sources of finance', in C. Darlow (ed.), *Valuation and Development Appraisal*, Estates Gazette, London.

Darlow, C. (1988b) 'Corporate and share capital funding', in C. Darlow (ed.), *Valuation and Development Appraisal*, Estates Gazette, London.

Darlow, C. (1988c) 'Direct project funding', in C. Darlow (ed.), *Valuation and Development Appraisal*, Estates Gazette, London.

Debenham, Tewson and Chinnocks (1984) *Property Investment in Britain*, Debenham, Tewson and Chinnocks, London.

DTZ Debenham Thorpe (1993) *Money into Property*, August, DTZ Debenham Thorpe, London.

Fraser, W. D. (1993) *Principles of Property Investment and Pricing*, Macmillan (now Palgrave), London.

Isaac, D. (1994) *Property Finance*, Macmillan (now Palgrave), London.

Isaac, D. and O'Grady, M. (1993) 'Thorough approach the key to development funding', *Property Valuer*, Winter, Dublin.

Jones, T. and Isaac, D. (1994) 'Finance for the smaller building company and contractor', *Chartered Institute of Building Directory*, CIOB/Macmillan (now Palgrave), London.

Pike, R. and Neale, B. (1993) *Corporate Finance and Investment*, Prentice Hall, London.

Riley, M. and Isaac, D. (1993) 'Commercial property lending: confidence survey', *Journal of Property Finance*, Vol. 4, No. 3.

Riley, M. and Isaac, D. (1994) 'Property lending survey 1994', *Journal of Property Finance*, Vol. 5, No. 1, pp.45–51.

Ross, S. A., Westerfield, R. W. and Jaffe, J. F. (1993) *Corporate Finance*, Irwin, Boston MA.

Savills (1989) *Financing Property 1989*, Savills, London.

Savills (1993) *Financing Property 1993*, Savills, London.

Scott, I. P. (1992) 'Debt, liquidity and secondary trading in property debt', *Journal of Property Finance*, Vol. 3, No. 3, pp.347–55.

Venmore-Rowland, P. (1991) 'Vehicles for property investment', in P. Venmore-Rowland, P. Brandon and T. Mole (eds), *Investment, Procurement and Performance in Construction*, RICS, London.

15 Financial Management and Accounts

15.1 Company financial statements
15.2 Basic accounting concepts
15.3 Techniques for analysis
15.4 Information in property company accounts
15.5 The regulation of accounts

AIMS AND OBJECTIVES

This chapter looks at financial management and accounts. It provides examples of the main financial statements and explains how to analyse them.

15.1 COMPANY FINANCIAL STATEMENTS

For investment appraisal, a knowledge of accounts is essential, because this provides the analysis of the corporate entity and can be used to analyse the strength of tenants, business partners and companies that are being invested in. This chapter provides an outline of financial management for these purposes.

A company's financial statements are contained in the report sent to its shareholders. The report provides details of the operations of the company. It contains a Chairman's review which looks at the preceding year and prospects for the future. There is also a Directors' Report which comments on such matters as profits, dividends, fixed assets and finance, and includes the report of the auditors and a summary of the accounting policies of the company which can be useful in the analysis of the position of the firm. Accounting policies are important in the property sector in respect of asset valuation, and different bases will be used according to whether a property company is an investment or a trading company. Attached to the report are the financial statements. These financial statements would be:

- the profit and loss account;
- the balance sheet;
- notes to the accounts;

- current cost accounts;
- a statement of source and applications of funds;
- a statement of value added.

In addition it is now also necessary to provide:

- a consolidated statement of total recognised gains and losses;
- a cash flow statement;
- a note of historical costs, profits and losses.

These are to aid the understanding of the information.

The balance sheet and the profit and loss account are the main statements of the financial situation of the company. The balance sheet would be for an individual or group of companies, but if there were a parent company then this may also be included. The main accounts would be in accordance with historic cost conventions, but current cost accounts would attempt to take into account inflation of asset values. It is useful to remind ourselves at this stage of those particular groups who need to use published accounts, because it is their needs for information that will have to be satisfied. These are set out in Box 15.1.

BOX 15.1: THE USERS OF PUBLISHED ACCOUNTS

Who are the users of published accounts?

The equity investor group including existing and potential shareholders and holders of convertible securities, options or warrants.

The loan creditor group including existing and potential holders of debentures and loan stock, and providers of short-term secured and unsecured loans and finance.

The employee group including existing, potential and past employees.

The analyst–adviser group including financial analysts and journalists, economists, statisticians, researchers, trade unions, stockbrokers and other providers of advisory services such as credit rating agencies.

The business contact group including customers, trade creditors and suppliers and, in a different sense, competitors, business rivals, and those interested in mergers, amalgamations and takeovers.

The government including tax authorities, departments and agencies concerned with the supervision of commerce and industry, and local authorities.

The public including taxpayers, ratepayers, consumers, and other community and special interest groups such as political parties, consumer and environmental protection societies and regional pressure groups.   [Westwick, 1980]

The balance sheet

The balance sheet lists the balances of assets and liabilities as at the accounting date. As a result of the EU's fourth directive on company accounts, balance sheets are now to be in a standardised form. The balance sheets are built up from three categories of entry: assets, liabilities and shareholders' funds. Thus total assets are equal to the sum of shareholders' funds plus liabilities if one looks at the balance sheet from the point of view of the company; alternatively, from a shareholder's view, one can see that the difference between assets and liabilities is the shareholders funds:

Business view: assets = shareholders' funds + liabilities

Shareholders' view: assets − liabilities = shareholders' funds

Fixed assets + Net current assets (Current assets *less* Current liabilities) = Capital employed (Shareholders' funds + Long-term liabilities). This is a modification of the business view, taking current liabilities to the asset side of the equation. The balance sheet model of the firm is set out in Figure 15.1 to clarify these concepts.

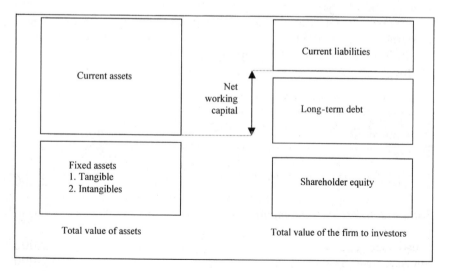

Figure 15.1   *The balance sheet model of the firm [Ross et al., 1993]*

Profit and loss account

While the balance sheet is for a particular moment, a profit and loss account is for a year ending on the accounting date – it is the result of the year's activities. The profit is shown before and after tax. Profit attributable to minority interests arises from investment in other companies that amounts to 50 per cent or less of ownership, and these profits are now allowed to be consolidated in the sheet. The accounts also show the proportion of profit distributed and retained. To grow, a company will need to increase its assets. The balance sheet shows that assets = liabilities *plus* shareholders' funds, so that the ways to grow would be to increase liabilities (borrow more) or increase shareholders' funds. There are two ways of increasing the shareholders' funds: by issuing more shares or ploughing back profits. Ploughing back profits is not necessarily the cheapest source of long-term funds for the company and it also restricts the payment of dividends.

Examples of a balance sheet and a profit and loss account

Balance sheet as at 31 March

	£'000	£'000
Fixed assets		
(investment properties for property companies)		3,000
Land and buildings for occupation		400
Plant and machinery		200
Fixtures and fittings		200
		3,800
Current assets		
Stocks (trading properties for property companies)	3,000	
Debtors	100	
Cash	100	
	3,200	
Current liabilities		
Bank overdraft	400	
Trade creditors	600	
	1,000	
Net current assets		2,200
Total assets less *current liabilities*		6,000
Capital and reserves		
Issued share capital		2,000
Revenue reserves		1,000
Capital reserves		1,000

Shareholders' interest	4,000
Long-term liabilities (over one year)	
Loans	2,000
Total long-term capital	6,000

(adapted from Asch and Kaye, 1989)

Notes to balance sheet

These notes refer to an ordinary trading company, notes relating to the peculiarities of property companies are in brackets.

Fixed assets

Assets were normally valued at historic cost for an ordinary company. Land and buildings were shown at original cost *less* depreciation in normal accounts but, because this does not reflect worth, companies now revalue to market value. Depreciation is an annual allowance for wear and tear and reduces the balance sheet valuation; it is deducted from profit as a cost. (For a property company, the valuation should be market value for an investment property or the lower of cost and realisable value for a property in the course of development, but intended as an investment property – that is, intended as a fixed asset.) Fixed assets are intended to be permanent features of the company's assets, current assets are turned into cash usually within one year. Plant and machinery and fixtures and fittings are shown at cost *less* depreciation.

Current assets

Stocks are valued at cost. (For a property company, properties to be traded are stocks and are valued at the lower of realisable value or cost.) Cost includes the expenses paid out on a property since purchase and interest.

Current liabilities

These are the amounts due to creditors within 1 year. The balance of current assets *less* current liabilities is called the 'net working capital'.

Capital and reserves

Issued share capital is the amount paid in by the shareholders when they originally bought the shares in the company. Reserves arise because profits are not distributed to shareholders but ploughed back in the company; these are called 'revenue reserves'. Revenue reserves have to be distinguished from capital reserves which arise on the revaluation of assets and which then may give rise to a surplus. (Capital reserves are especially important in property companies, as they arise from revaluation of the assets rather than profits from rents or trading.)

Long-term liabilities
These are amounts owed by the company at a future date, longer than one year.

Profit and loss account for the year ended 31 March

		£'000	£'000
Turnover			10,000
Less Cost of sales (direct costs)			6,500
Gross profit			3,500
Less (indirect costs)	Administration expenses	1,000	
	Selling and distribution costs	200	
	Interest on loans	150	
			1,350
Net profit before tax			2,150
Corporation tax			750
Profit on ordinary activities after tax			1,400
Extraordinary item after taxation			200
Profit for the year			1,200
Dividends			600
Transfer to reserves			600

[Asch and Kaye, 1989]

Notes to profit and loss account

Whereas the balance sheet reveals the state of affairs of the company at one point in time, the profit and loss account shows how much net cash has been generated by activities over the accounting period by matching the expenditure of the year against the revenues. The cost of sales are the cost of raw materials, production or direct labour, power and other factory costs. An extraordinary item is one that is unusual in terms of size and frequency. They are infrequent and thus need to be omitted when considering profit trends over a period of years; for instance, a large profit may have been made from disposal of part of the business, an event which is unlikely to occur again and which distorts the profit figure for that year.

15.2 BASIC ACCOUNTING CONCEPTS

The financial statements are produced and based on accounting concepts. Four rules or concepts are observed in all published accounts, unless it is otherwise stated. These rules are:

- the going concern concept;
- the accruals concept;
- the consistency concept;
- the prudence concept.

The going concern concept assumes that the business will be continuing its activities for the foreseeable future on a similar scale. Thus the values attaching to assets and liabilities in the Balance Sheet reflect going concern values. This concept is important in property asset valuation for accounts purposes. The accruals concept says that it is vital for an accurate assessment of profit and loss for the accounting period to compare costs and benefits accurately. It is important to assign costs and financial returns to the period incurred, which may not be the same time period when money costs are incurred or financial returns received. For instance, if a sale has legally taken place, whether or not cash has been received from the customer for the goods delivered, the transaction will be taken as a sale and included as part of the sales revenue appearing in the profit and loss account. The consistency concept is necessary so that approaches to the formulation of the accounts remain the same and so that valid comparisons and analysis can be made against previous results and with other companies. The prudence concept covers the attitudes of dealing with costs and revenues; it is the cautious way that an accountant approaches the problem, unless it is certain. Based on the above concepts, the Companies Acts makes it a legal requirement that a company's Balance Sheet should show a true and fair view.

15.3 TECHNIQUES FOR ANALYSIS

The analysis of company accounts involves the initial consideration of three problems:

1. Is the company making a satisfactory profit?
2. Is the company short of cash or cash rich?
3. What should be the source of long-term funds?

These problems relate to profitability, liquidity and capital structure, and are as applicable to individual property projects as they are to property companies or any firm. The techniques applied are based on relationships between the elements in the financial statements (financial ratios) and rates of return (yields). The area of capital structure is of major interest in financing arrangements and has parallels in the financial construction of property projects.

Profitability measures

The key ratios used to analyse the profitability of an enterprise are:

1. Trading profit as a percentage of turnover.
2. Profit before interest and tax as a percentage of average capital employed.
3. Earnings per share, either basic (based on issued share capital) or fully diluted (based on authorised share capital, which is the total share capital that can be issued).
4. Dividend per share.
5. Number of times covered – that is, the number of times a dividend is covered by earnings. This is also a measure used by property managers to assess the security of a tenant by calculating the number of times the rent is covered by the net profit of the tenant company.
6. Assets per share – the asset backing of shares based on the value of the net assets divided by the number of shares. There has been much discussion in this area in relation to the share price of property investment companies, as one would expect the asset value per share to relate to the market price of the share. However, traditionally the market has discounted the net asset values of property investment companies historically by an average of approximately 20 per cent. The discount is measured by:

$$\frac{\text{Share price} - \text{Net asset value per share}}{\text{Net asset value per share}} \times 100 \text{ per cent}$$

[Isaac and Woodroffe, 1987]

Return on investment

This is defined as:

$$\frac{\text{Profit}}{\text{Assets}} \times 100 \text{ per cent}$$

Thus profit is looked at as a percentage of capital and this is further influenced by two further ratios comprising the profit margin (profit as a percentage of sales) and the rate of asset turnover (sales dividend by assets).

$$\frac{\text{Profit}}{\text{Assets}} = \frac{\text{Profit}}{\text{Sales}} \times \frac{\text{Sales}}{\text{Assets}}$$

or   Return on capital = profit margin × turnover

The return on capital may vary from one industry to another but wider variations may be found in the profit margin and rates of turnover. For instance, a return of 20 per cent could be achieved by a high profit margin and a low turnover (the corner shop), or a low profit margin and a high turnover (the supermarket piling the goods high and selling cheap).

A sector comparison should show that capital-intensive industries with long production cycles have a low rate of turnover but a high profit margin. From the key ratios above, a number of subsidiary ratios relating costs or assets to sales can be formulated. Depending on the use to which the ratio is put, the definition of profit and assets will differ. Generally a wider view of company performance is taken:

$$\text{Return on capital} = \frac{\text{Profit before tax, interest and dividends}}{\text{Total capital employed}}$$

The comparison of profitable ratios enables firms within a sector to be compared against one another, and for the various sectors to be compared.

Liquidity and cash flows

As well as being profitable, it is also important that a company should be liquid. A profitable and fast expanding company may find that it has tied up its profits in fixed assets, stocks and debtors, and that is has difficulty paying its debts as they fall due. There are two main ratios to examine the liquidity of a company: the liquidity ratio and the current ratio.

The *liquidity ratio* is also called the 'acid test ratio' because it is a most important test. It is the ratio of liquid assets to current liabilities, and a $1:1$ ratio means that a company has sufficient cash to pay its immediate debts. Liquid assets are defined as current assets excluding stocks of goods which cannot be quickly turned into cash. In effect, liquid assets are debtors, cash and any short-term investments such as bank deposits or government securities. A company can survive with a liquid ratio of less than $1:1$ if it has an unused bank overdraft facility.

The other test of a company's liquidity is the *current ratio*, which includes stocks and work in progress on the grounds that stocks eventually turn into debtors and then into cash itself. It is calculated by relating all current assets to current liabilities. A norm of $2:1$ is generally regarded as being satisfactory, but this will depend on the norm for a particular industry. Thus

Liquidity ratio = Liquid assets : Current liabilities

Current ratio = Current assets : Current liabilities

Gearing ratio and interest cover

Two important measures of financial analysis are the gearing ratio and interest cover, as shown in Example 15.1.

The *gearing* (or leverage) *ratio* is the ratio of debt to shareholders' funds.
This could be expressed as the ratio of debt to net operating assets, and this
is the approach used in most economic texts, but normally in the market it
is stated as:

$$\text{Gearing ratio} = \frac{\text{Debt (borrowings)}}{\text{Shareholders' funds}}$$

also known as the debt to equity ratio.

Interest cover is the profit available to pay interest charges:

$$\text{Interest cover} = \frac{\text{Profit before interest and tax}}{\text{Net interest}}$$

Example 15.1: Gearing ratio and interest cover

	Company A £m	Company B £m
Balance Sheet		
Net operating assets	100	100
Financed by: Debt	20	80
Shareholders	80	20
	100	100
Profit and Loss Account		
Operating profit	15.0	15.0
Less Interest payable @ 10 per cent	(2.0)	(8.0)
Profit before tax	13.0	7.0
Tax @ 35 per cent	(4.55)	(2.5)
Net profit	8.45	4.5
Gearing ratio	$\frac{20}{80} = 25$ per cent	$\frac{80}{20} = 400$ per cent
Interest cover	$\frac{15}{2} = 7.5$ times	$\frac{15}{8} = 1.88$ times

The gearing ratio is used to compare levels of debt between companies. Interest cover indicates the safety margin before profits become inadequate to cover the interest charge. Gearing and interest cover are used by lenders to determine whether a company's borrowings are at a reasonable level and whether it is prudent to lend more.

Investors are concerned with the company's capacity to absorb a decrease in profit without having to sell assets in possible unfavourable market conditions. Also, gearing is a measure of the potential to finance expansion without recourse to the shareholders, which would depress share price. If a company requires additional debt to fund a new project, the resultant gearing effect may depress share price and restrict flexibility to respond to future opportunities. There is thus pressure to record the project, the asset and debt off-balance sheet.

Analysing a property company – a summary

In order to analyse a property company, its accounts and finances, the following criteria will be important:

1. *Net asset value per share.* If the net assets are £10 million and the issued share capital is 5 million shares at £1 each, then the net asset value per share is £10 million/5 million, i.e. £2 or 200p per share.
2. *Gearing.* If the shareholders' funds are £5 million and the debt capital is £3 million, then the gearing is £3 million/£5 million, i.e. 0.66 or 66 per cent.
3. *Composition of interest rates in the debt.* What is the percentage of variable rate loans to total loans? A company with a lot of debt with floating rates may find its share price suffering, especially in a period of volatile interest rates.
4. *Valuation of assets.* When were they last valued? Property companies are meant to value their properties internally annually and have an external independent valuation every five years.
5. *Comparison of the amount of properties shown at cost* (development properties in the process of being developed) *with the amount shown at value* (investment property). This analysis gives an indication of the level of development activity.
6. *The legal interests in properties held.* The breakdown of properties into freeholds, long leaseholds and short leaseholds can give an indication of the type and amount of income arising and the nature of the reviews.
7. *Comparison of profit.* A year-on-year comparison, excluding extraordinary items, is a valuable analysis.

8. *Capital*. How is it financed? What capital commitments are there?
9. *Contingent liabilities*. Has the company guaranteed the borrowing of associate companies which increases its liabilities? Are there any off-balance sheet transactions?   [Adapted from Brett, 1990b].

15.4   INFORMATION IN PROPERTY COMPANY ACCOUNTS

In May 1990, chartered accountants Stoy Hayward and researchers from the University of Reading set up a panel of experts to look at the provision of information in property company accounts and the main areas of problems relating to loans and interest, the nature of the assets and joint ventures. The recommendations of the panel are listed below:

1. Property company accounts should be placed in context, in terms of: what has happened over the year; how the company has been performing over the last five years; a view of the future; and what accounting policies are used.
2. More details should be included about loan arrangements, the payment of interest and the capitalisation of interest.
3. An analysis of properties should be included, showing their use as either trading stock, investment properties or development properties.
4. A list of properties with a worth greater than 5 per cent of the total property portfolio should be included.
5. An external revaluation, on an open-market basis, should be carried out in accordance with the guidelines of the Royal Institution of Chartered Surveyors.
6. All revaluation gains or losses should be passed into a property revaluation reserve, shown in the accounts as a capital profit and loss account which distinguishes between realised and unrealised amounts.
7. Details of costs and revenues from all developments relating to, and details of, all joint ventures should be included.   [Purdy, 1992]

15.5   THE REGULATION OF ACCOUNTS

There are several sources of regulation with which statutory accounts have to comply. These are:

1. The Companies Acts, which describe the principles which should be followed in preparing statutory accounts. They indicate that accounts should show a true and fair view. The Companies Acts also set out the detailed disclosure requirements.

2. The accounting profession publishes SSAPs (Statements of Standard Accounting Practice) and these cover accounting and disclosure.
3. If the company is listed, the Stock Exchange specifies mandatory disclosure requirements.

The company accounts are independently examined by the auditor who has to report to the shareholders that the accounts show a true and fair view and are properly prepared in accordance with the Companies Act. Auditors are under a professional obligation to ensure the accounts comply with SSAPs. If the accounts do not accord with the regulations, the auditor must state this in his report unless, in exceptional circumstances, he concurs with a departure from an SSAP. This seldom happens. If the auditor is going to qualify the accounts, he will discuss this with the directors and often they will amend the accounts to avoid qualification. The auditor will also advise of any failure to observe the relevant requirements of the Stock Exchange.

Exercise question

What are the main components of the balance sheet. Distinguish between assets and liabilities and show how working capital may be calculated.

Outline answer

You need to examine the various elements of the Balance Sheet and give examples of the different items. It is important to distinguish between fixed and current assets, and long-term and current liabilities. For instance, fixed assets are held by the business for use rather than resale, and may be held for a number of years. Current assets include assets that are already cash or that are intended to be turned back into cash in the course of trading activity. The capital employed in a business is used for the purchase of fixed assets or for working capital. Working capital is the value of the current assets of a business *less* the current liabilities.

SUMMARY OF CHAPTER

This chapter has looked at financial management and accounts and has covered the following specific areas:

- Financial statements.
- The analysis of the statements.

- Information contained in the statements.
- The regulation of accounts.

REFERENCES AND BIBLIOGRAPHY

Accounting Standards Committee (ASC) (1990) *Exposure Draft 51, Accounting for fixed assets and revaluations*, May, ASC.

Asch, D. and Kaye, G. R. (1989) *Financial Planning: Modelling Methods and Techniques*, Kogan Paul, London.

Barkham, R. J. and Purdy, D. E. (1992) 'Financial company reporting: potential weaknesses', *Journal of Property Valuation and Investment*, Vol. 11, No. 2, pp.133–44.

Brett, M. (1990a) *Property and Money*, Estates Gazette, London.

Brett, M. (1990b) *How to read the financial pages*, Hutchison, London.

Calachi, R. and Rosenburg, S. (eds) (1992) *Property Finance, An International Perspective*, Euromoney Books, London.

Isaac, D. (1994) *Property Finance*, Macmillan (now Palgrave), London.

Isaac, D. and Woodroffe, N. (1987) 'Are property company assets undervalued', *Estates Gazette*, London, 5 September, pp.1024–6.

Parker, R. H. (1982) *Understanding Company Financial Statements*, Pelican, London.

Peat, M. (1988) 'The Accounting Issues', in S. L. Barter (ed.), *Real Estate Finance*, Butterworths, London.

Pike, R. and Neale, B. (1993) *Corporate Finance and Investment*, Prentice Hall, London.

Purdy, D. E. (1992) 'Provoking awareness through the provision of relevant information in property company accounts', *Journal of Property Finance*, Vol. 3, No. 3, pp.337–46.

Ross, S. A., Westerfield, R. W. and Jaffe, J. F. (1993) *Corporate Finance*, Irwin, Boston MA.

Ryland, D. S. (1992) 'Changes in accounting rules', *Journal of Property Finance*, Vol. 3, No. 1, pp.28–37.

Smee, R. (1992) 'Capitalisation of interest for property companies', *Journal of Property Finance*, Vol. 3, No. 1, pp.13–22.

Westwick, C. A. (1980) *Property Valuation and Accounts*, Institute of Chartered Accountants in England and Wales, London.

Bibliography

Accounting Standards Committee (ASC) (1990) *Exposure Draft 51, Accounting for fixed assets and revaluations*, May, ASC.

Asch, D. and Kaye, G. R. (1989) *Financial Planning: Modelling Methods and Techniques*, Kogan Paul, London.

Balchin, P. and Bull, G. (1987) *Regional and Urban Economics*, Harper & Row, London.

Balchin, P. N., Isaac, D. and Chen, J. (2000) *Urban Economics: A Global Perspective*, Palgrave, Basingstoke, Hants/New York.

Bank of England (1994) *Quarterly Bulletin*, Vol. 34, No. 3, August.

Bank of England (1994) *Quarterly Bulletin*, Vol. 34, No. 4, November.

Bank of England (1996) *Quarterly Bulletin*, Vol. 36, No. 4, November.

Barkham, R. J. and Purdy, D. E. (1992) 'Financial company reporting: potential weaknesses', *Journal of Property Valuation and Investment*, Vol. 11, No. 2, pp.133–44.

Barkham, R. J., Ward, C. W. R. and Henry, O. T. (1995) 'The inflation-hedging characteristics of UK property', *Journal of Property Finance*, Vol. 7, No. 1, pp.62–76.

Barkshire, R. (1986) *The Unitised Property Market*, February, Working Party of the Unitised Property Market, London.

Barras, R. (1994) 'Property and the economic cycle: building cycles revisited', *Journal of Property Research*, Vol. 11, No. 3, winter, pp.183–97.

Barter, S. L. (1988) 'Introduction', in S. L. Barter (ed.), *Real Estate Finance*, Butterworths, London.

Baum, A. and Crosby, N. (1988) *Property Investment Appraisal*, Routledge, London.

Baum, A. and Crosby, N. (1995) *Property Investment Appraisal*, Routledge, London.

Baum, A., Crosby, N. and MacGregor, B. (1996) 'Price formation, mispricing and investment analysis in the property market. A response to "A note on The initial yield revealed: explicit valuations and the future of property investment"', *Journal of Property Valuation and Investment*, Vol. 14, No. 1, pp.36–49.

Baum, A. E. (1989) 'A critical examination of the measurement of property investment and risk appraisal', *Discussion Paper Series*, No. 22, April, University of Cambridge, Department of Land Economy.

Baum, A. E. and Schofield, A. (1991) 'Property as a global asset', in P. Venmore-Rowland, P. Brandon and T. Mole (eds), *Investment, Procurement and Performance in Construction*, RICS, London.

Beveridge, J. A. (1991) 'New methods of financing', in P. Venmore-Rowland, P. Brandon and T. Mole (eds), *Investment, Procurement and Performance in Construction*, RICS, London.

Brett, M. (1983) 'Growth of financial institutions', in C. Darlow (ed.), *Valuation and Investment Appraisal*, Estates Gazette, London.

Brett, M. (1983) 'Indirect Investment in Property', in C. Darlow (ed.), *Valuation and Investment Appraisal*, Estates Gazette, London.

Brett, M. (1989) 'Characteristics of property', *Estates Gazette*, 21 January, p.14.

Brett, M. (1990) *How to read the financial pages*, Hutchison, London.

Brett, M. (1990) *Property and Money*, Estates Gazette, London.

Brett, M. (1997) *Property and Money*, Estates Gazette, London.

Britton, W., Davies, K. and Johnson, T. (1990) *Modern Methods of Valuation*, Estates Gazette, London.

Brown, G. R. (1991) *Property Investment and the Capital Markets*, E. & F. N. Spon, London.

Butler, D. (1995) *Applied Valuation*, Macmillan (now Palgrave), London.

Butler, D. and Richmond, D. (1990) *Advanced Valuation*, Macmillan (now Palgrave), London.

Byrne, P. and Cadman, D. (1984) *Risk, Uncertainty and Decision Making in Property Development*, E. & F. N. Spon, London.

Calachi, R. and Rosenburg, S. (eds) (1992) *Property Finance, An International Perspective*, Euromoney Books, London.

Central Statistical Office (CSO) (1992) *Financial Statistics: Explanatory Handbook*, December, CSO.

Central Statistical Office (CSO) (1993) *Financial Statistics*, September, CSO.

Central Statistical Office (CSO) (1993) *Housing and Construction Statistics*, September, CSO.

Central Statistical Office (CSO) (1994) *Economic Trends*, HMSO, London.

Central Statistical Office (CSO) (1994) *Financial Statistics*, November, CSO.

Central Statistical Office (CSO) (1995) *UK Economic Accounts*, No. 8, January, HMSO, London.

Central Statistical Office (CSO) (1996) *Annual Abstract of Statistics: 1996 Edition*, HMSO, London.

Central Statistical Office (CSO) (1996) *Financial Statistics*, November, CSO.

Chapman, C. B. (1991) 'Risk', in P. Venmore-Rowland, P. Brandon and T. Mole (eds), *Investment, Procurement and Performance in Construction*, RICS, London.

Chartered Surveyor Monthly (CSM) (1995) 'Finding your way into the new Red Book', *Chartered Surveyor Monthly*, October, p.22.

Chartered Surveyor Monthly (CSM) (1995) 'Finding your way into the new Red Book', *Chartered Surveyor Monthly*, November/December, pp.20–2.

Chartered Surveyor Monthly (CSM) (1995) 'Mallinson delivers a yorker', *Chartered Surveyor Monthly*, November/December, p.48.

Chartered Surveyor Monthly (CSM) (1996) 'The variable value of property investment valuation reports', *Chartered Surveyor Monthly*, April, pp.38–9.

Chartered Surveyor Monthly (CSM) (2000) 'Useful websites for surveyors', *Chartered Surveyor Monthly*, February, p.23.

Chesterton Financial (1995) *Property Lending Survey*, February, Chesterton Financial, London.

Chesterton Financial/CSW (1993) *Property Confidence Barometer*, July, Chesterton Financial, London.

Colborne, A. (1992) *Profits Method*, paper presented at RICS Valuation Techniques Seminar, 13 March.

Connellan, O. (1992) *Cost Approach to Valuation*, paper presented at RICS Valuation Techniques Seminar, 13 March.

Copeland, T. E. and Weston, J. F. (1988) *Financial Theory and Corporate Policy*, Addison-Wesley, Wokingham, Berks.

Crosby, N. (1991) 'Over-rented freehold investment property valuation', *Journal of Property Valuation and Investment*, Vol. 10, No. 2, pp.517–24.

Crosby, N. (1992) *Reversionary Freeholds; UK Market Valuation Practice*, Research paper, RICS, London.

Crosby, N. and Goodchild, R. (1992) 'Reversionary freeholds: problems with over-renting', *Journal of Property Valuation and Investment*, Vol. 11, No. 1, pp.67–81.

Currie, D. and Scott, A. (1991) *The Place of Commercial Property in the UK Economy*, January, London Business School.

D J Freeman (1994) *The Language of Property Finance*, D J Freeman, London.

Darlow, C. (ed.) (1983) *Valuation and Investment Appraisal*, Estates Gazette, London.

Darlow, C. (ed.) (1988) *Valuation and Development Appraisal*, Estates Gazette, London.

Darlow, C. (1988) 'Corporate and share capital funding', in C. Darlow (ed.), *Valuation and Development Appraisal*, Estates Gazette, London.

Darlow, C. (1988) 'Direct project funding', in C. Darlow (ed.), *Valuation and Development Appraisal*, Estates Gazette, London.

Darlow, C. (1988) 'The supply and sources of finance', in C. Darlow (ed.), *Valuation and Development Appraisal*, Estates Gazette, London.

Davidson, A. W. (1989) *Parry's Valuation and Investment Tables*, Estates Gazette, London.

Debenham, Tewson and Chinnocks (1984) *Property Investment in Britain*, Debenham, Tewson and Chinnocks, London.

DoE (Department of the Environment) (1994) *Housing and Construction Statistics 1982–1993 (Great Britain)*, HMSO, London.

DoE (Department of the Environment) (1994) *Housing and Construction Statistics (Great Britain)*, June quarter 1994, part 2, HMSO, London.

Drivers Jonas/IPD (1988) *The Variance in Valuations*, Autumn, Drivers Jonas Research Department, London.

DTZ Debenham Thorpe (1993) *Money into Property*, August, DTZ Debenham Thorpe, London.

DTZ Debenham Thorpe (1996) *Money into Property*, September, DTZ Debenham Thorpe, London.

Dubben, N. and Sayce, S. (1991) *Property Portfolio Management: An Introduction*, Routledge, London.

Enever, N. and Isaac, D. (1995) *The Valuation of Property Investments*, Estates Gazette, London.

Estates Gazette (1995) 'Mainly for students: spreadsheets and valuations', *Estates Gazette*, 21 January, pp.116–19.

Estates Gazette (1995) 'Property cycles explained', *Estates Gazette*, 25 November, pp.147–8.

Estates Gazette (1996) 'The new Red Book', *Estates Gazette*, 6 January, pp.96–7.

Estates Times (1993) 'Swaps not cash', *Estates Times*, 19 November, p.24.

Evans, P. H. (1993) 'Statistical review', *Journal of Property Finance*, Vol. 4, No. 2, pp.75–82.

Fisher, I. (1930) *The Theory of Interest*, Porcupine Press, Philadephia PA.

Fraser, W. (1996) 'A schematic model of the commercial property market', *Chartered Surveyor Monthly*, January, pp.32–3.

Fraser, W. D. (1993) *Principles of Property Investment and Pricing*, Macmillan (now Palgrave), London.

French, N. (1994) 'Editorial: market values & DCF', *Journal of Property Valuation and Investment*, Vol. 12, No. 1, pp.4–6.

French, N. and Ward, C. (1995) 'Valuation and arbitrage', *Journal of Property Research*, Vol. 12, No. 1, Spring, pp.1–11.

Gibbs, R. (1987) 'Raising finance for new development', *Journal of Valuation*, Vol. 5, No. 4, pp.343–53.

Hargitay, S. E. and Sui-Ming Yu (1993) *Property Investment Decisions*, E. & F. N. Spon, London.

Investment Property Databank (IPD) (1992) *Annual Review: 1993*, December, IPD Ltd, London.

International Property Databank (IPD) (1996) *Annual Index: 1995*, IPD Ltd, London.

International Property Databank (IPD) (1996) *Monthly Index:* September, IPD Ltd, London.

International Property Databank (IPD) (2000) *IPD UK Annual Index*, March, IPD Ltd, London.

Isaac, D. (1994) *Property Finance*, Macmillan (now Palgrave), London.

Isaac, D. (1996) *Property Development: Appraisal and Finance*, Macmillan (now Palgrave), London.

Isaac, D. and Steley, T. (2000) *Property Valuation Techniques*, Macmillan (now Palgrave), London.

Isaac, D. and Woodroffe, N. (1987) 'Are property company assets undervalued?', *Estates Gazette*, 5 September, pp.1024–6.

Isaac, D. and Woodroffe, N. (1995) *Property Companies: Share Price and Net Asset Value*, Greenwich University Press, London.

Jenkins, S. (1996) 'Valuations still highly variable', *Estates Times*, 15 March, p.2.

Jones Lang Wotton (1989) *The Glossary of Property Terms*, Estates Gazette, London.

Keogh, G. (1994) 'Use and investment markets in British real estate', *Journal of Property Valuation and Investment*, Vol. 12, No. 4, pp.58–72.

Law, D. and Gershinson, J. (1995) 'Whatever happened to ERP?', *Estates Gazette*, 16 September, pp.164–5.

Lennox, K. (1996) 'Thumbs up for property: IPF/EG survey', *Estates Gazette*, 20 April, p.41.

Lumby, S. (1991) *Investment Appraisal and Financing Decisions*, Chapman & Hall, London.

Mallinson, M. (1988) 'Equity finance', in S. L. Barter (ed.), *Real Estate Finance*, Butterworths, London.

Matysiak, G., Hoesli, M., MacGregor, B. and Nanthakumaran, N. (1995) 'Long-term inflation-hedging characteristics of UK commercial property', *Journal of Property Finance*, Vol. 7, No. 1, pp.50–61.

Millington, A. F. (1984) *An Introduction to Property Valuation*, Estates Gazette, London.

Millman, S. (1988) 'Property, property companies and public securities', in S. L. Barter (ed.), *Real Estate Finance*, Butterworths, London.

Morley, S. (1988) 'Financial appraisal – cashflow approach', in C. Darlow (ed.), *Valuation and Development Appraisal*, Estates Gazette, London.

Morley, S. (1988) 'Financial appraisal – sensitivity and probability', in C. Darlow (ed.), *Valuation and Development Appraisal*, Estates Gazette, London.

Morley, S. J. E. (1988) 'The analysis of risk in the appraisal of property investment', in A. R. MacLeary and N. Nanthakumaran (eds), *Property Investment Theory*, E. & F. N. Spon, London.

Peat, M. (1988) 'The accounting issues', in S. L. Barter (ed.), *Real Estate Finance*, Butterworths, London.

Peto, R., French, N. and Bowman, G. (1996) 'Price and worth: developments in valuation methodology', *Journal of Property Valuation and Investment*, Vol. 14, No. 4, pp.79–100.

Pike, R. and Neale, B. (1993) *Corporate Finance and Investment*, Prentice Hall, London.

Pugh, C. (1991) 'The globalisation of finance capital and the changing relationships between property and finance', *Journal of Property Finance*, Vol. 2, No. 2, pp.211–15 and No. 3, pp.369–79.

Pugh, C. and Dehesh, A. (1995) 'International property cycles: the causes', *Chartered Surveyor Monthly*, January, p.33.

Purdy, D. E. (1992) 'Provoking awareness through the provision of relevant information in property company accounts', *Journal of Property Finance*, Vol. 3, No. 3, pp.337–46.

Rayner, M. (1988) *Asset Valuation*, Macmillan (now Palgrave), London.

Rees, W. H. (ed.) (1992) *Valuation: Principles into Practice*, Estates Gazette, London.

Rich, J. (1994) 'The wonderland of OMVs, ERPs and DAVs', *Estates Gazette*, 26 November, pp.153–5.

Riley, M. and Isaac, D. (1994) 'Property lending survey 1994', *Journal of Property Finance*, Vol. 5, No. 1, pp.45–51.

Riley, M. and Isaac, D. (1995) 'Property lending survey 1995', *Journal of Property Finance*, Vol. 6, No. 1, pp.67–72.

Ross, S. A., Westerfield, R. W. and Jaffe, J. F. (1993) *Corporate Finance*, Irwin, Boston MA.

Royal Institution of Chartered Surveyors (RICS) (1992) *Statement of Asset Valuation Practice and Guidance Notes*, RICS, London.

Royal Institution of Chartered Surveyors (RICS) (1994) *President's Working Party on Commercial Property Valuations (Mallinson Report)*, March, RICS, London.

Royal Institution of Chartered Surveyors (RICS) (1994) *Understanding the Property Cycle: Economic Cycles and Property Cycles*, May, RICS, London.

Royal Institution of Chartered Surveyors (RICS) (1995) *RICS Appraisal and Valuation Manual*, RICS, London.

Royal Institution of Chartered Surveyors (RICS) (1995) *Trade Related Valuations and Goodwill*, Guidance Note 7, RICS, London.

Rydin, Y., Rodney, W. and Orr, C. (1990) 'Why do institutions invest in property?', *Journal of Property Finance*, Vol. 1, No. 2, pp.250–8.

Ryland, D. S. (1992) 'Changes in accounting rules', *Journal of Property Finance*, Vol. 3, No. 1, pp.28–37.

Savills (1989) *Financing Property 1989*, Savills, London.

Savills (1993) *Financing Property 1993*, Savills, London.

Savills (1993) *Investment and Economic Outlook*, Issue 3, October, Savills, London.

Scarrett, D. (1991) *Property Valuation: The Five Methods*, E. & F. N. Spon, London.

Schiller, R. (1990) 'International property investment: the importance of debt', *Estates Gazette*, 24 February, pp.22–4.

Scott, I. P. (1992) 'Debt, liquidity and secondary trading in property debt', *Journal of Property Finance*, Vol. 3, No. 3, pp.347–55.

Seeley, I. H. (1996) *Building Economics*, Macmillan (now Palgrave), London.

Sweeney, F. (1988) '20% in property – a viable strategy', *Estates Gazette*, 13 February, pp.26–8.

The Times (2000) 'Gordon stamps all over Cabinet colleagues', *The Times*, 22 March, p.39.

Valuation Office (VO) (1998) *Property Market Review*, Autumn, VO.

Waldy, E. B. D. (1991) 'Single asset risk', in P. Venmore-Rowland, P. Brandon and T. Mole (eds), *Investment, Procurement and Performance in Construction*, RICS, London.

Watson, C. J., Billingsley, P., Croft, D. J. and Huntsberger, D. V. (1990) *Statistics for Management and Economics*, Allyn and Bacon, Boston MA.

Westwick, C. A. (1980) *Property Valuation and Accounts*, Institute of Chartered Accountants in England and Wales, London.

Woodroffe, N. and Isaac, D. (1987) 'Corporate finance and property development funding', *Working Paper of the School of Applied Economics and Social Studies*, Faculty of the Built Environment, South Bank Polytechnic, London.

Wright, M. G. (1990) *Using Discounted Cash Flow in Investment Appraisal*, McGraw-Hill, London.

Index